NO TEARS
FOR THE GENERAL

NO TEARS
FOR THE GENERAL

The Life of Alfred Sully, 1821–1879

by Langdon Sully

Foreword by Ray Allen Billington

WESTERN BIOGRAPHY SERIES

AMERICAN WEST PUBLISHING COMPANY
PALO ALTO—CALIFORNIA

OTHER WESTERN BIOGRAPHY SERIES BOOKS

Hippocrates in a Red Vest

My Dear Wister

Journeys to the Far North

Thrashin' Time

Library of Congress Card Number 73-90794
ISBN 0-910118-33-7

To the two Mary Sullys,
my late mother and my devoted wife
—without their active help and encouragement
it would not have been possible for me to
put this book together.

Contents

Foreword

by Ray Allen Billington

Occasionally—very occasionally—unpublished diaries or letters come to light that not only add details to the mosaic of history but do so in a prose style that captures the spirit of their day. On even rarer occasions—so rare as to be almost unique—those records have been written by an artist as gifted with the brush as he is with the pen, capable of supplying illustrative gems that add glamor and realism to his story. The letters of Alfred Sully, printed for the first time in this book, belong in that category. They offer us a vivid word picture of California during its gold rush period, of the western frontier in the 1850s, of the peninsula campaign of the Civil War, of the Sioux uprising of the 1860s. They also provide a medium for a sizeable number of the hundred-odd paintings and sketches that Sully prepared during his travels, paintings and sketches that give us a fresh look at many of the scenes and people described in the letters. The result is a volume as appealing to the eye as it is enlightening to the mind.

Alfred Sully inherited both his literary skill and his artistic talents from his well-known father, the artist Thomas Sully. Raised in the family home in Philadelphia amidst abundant cultural opportunities, young Sully's mechanical ingenuity suggested a career in engineering rather than painting. West Point was the logical training ground for those with such a bent, and there he enrolled, graduating with few distinctions in 1841. For a time Sully served with the forces that wrote a tragic end to Florida's Seminole War, then in the Mexican War where he

9

served at the siege of Veracruz. During these campaigns he was too busy learning to be a soldier to begin the series of letters that were to illuminate his later years.

These began just after the Mexican War when he was ordered to garrison duty in California. There he arrived in the spring of 1849 after a miserable trip around Cape Horn, just as the first of the Forty Niners were turning that peaceful land into a shambles of greed and speculation. And there he lived for the next four years largely in Monterey and the fort at Benicia, but with frequent visits to San Francisco and occasional journeys to Santa Barbara. There he married the lovely Manuela, and there he endured the agonies of the damned as first she, and then their month-old baby died. All this time he wrote letters—long, full letters—to his sister Blanche. They told of his own hopes and his own despair; they graphically described the monotony and boredom of garrison duty, they pictured the emergence of California from a land of gold-inspired chaos to one of lusty young growth; they recounted the cultural conflicts—and the cultural accommodations—of a young officer so intrigued with Mexican civilization that he occasionally signed his name "Alfredo." These are the letters that form the bulk of this book and that provide us a fresh and extremely informative look at California during its formative years.

Sully's letters were less full and less frequent when he was transferred from California to the upper Mississippi Valley; most of the 1850s he spent at Fort Ridgely in Minnesota Territory and Fort Pierre in Nebraska Territory, building the outposts that would guard the advance of settlement, suffering the boredom of garrison duty, and developing into a first-rate soldier whose respect for Indians made him an unusually fine guardian of the borderlands. With the outbreak of the Civil War he was ordered to Washington, where he spent some months seeking transfer to combat duty before winning a spot under Gen. George B. McClellan. Then came fighting to satisfy the most ambitious officer: the Battle of Fair Oaks, the second Battle of Bull Run,

Fredericksburg, the peninsula campaign. Sully was a good soldier, even though he had hitched his wagon to the falling star of General McClellan, and fought with such distinction that within a few months he advanced from captain to brigadier general.

The outbreak of the Sioux War in Minnesota in 1862 opened another chapter in his career. Sully was too familiar with that frontier to be wasted in the East; in 1863 he was transferred to that theater where he led expeditions that scattered the Indians at White Stone Hill and Kildeer. Although worn by soldiering and so ill that he could not leave his tent at times, he insisted in pressing on to the Yellowstone, knowing that the Sioux and their allies would regroup unless completely chastised. That was Sully's last major campaign. In 1866 he married for the second time and settled into a routine of life in western posts that lasted until his death in 1879 at the age of fifty eight.

Alfred Sully earned few distinctions during his lifetime as an officer, but he typified the unsung heroes who preserved the Union during the Civil War and opened its gates for expansion during the years that followed. He won no plaudits, and in his later years suffered the sight of younger, less competent men enjoying promotions that he wanted for himself. Sometimes he was bitter and sometimes his letters overflowed with complaints. Why should he earn a pittance that would scarcely keep him in rations in California when speculators all about him were garnering fortunes? Why should he command incompetent militiamen in Oregon who were paid eight dollars a day when his own long-suffering regulars received only seven dollars a month? Why should he stay in the army when his repeated requests for leaves needed to restore his health were denied? Sully grumbled, but Sully stayed with the colors. He was a good soldier, and deserves a larger role in history than historians have accorded him.

Fortunately for posterity, he not only remained in military service but found time to write and sketch as he moved from post to post or from combat to combat. The result is a literary and artistic legacy of genuine significance. Sully was a born letter writer because he was a competent observer; he wrote warmly, vividly, of events that would have escaped the notice of less alert visitors. He was also a competent artist, less gifted than his father and inclined toward primitivism, but conveying a sense of realism that adds conviction to western scenes. Taken together his letters and drawings offer a unique view of the Old West, and particularly of California during its birth pangs.

Alfred Sully's grandson, Langdon Sully, who has made this handsome book possible, has been wise enough to let his ancestor tell most of the story. He has not produced a volume of documents in the traditional sense, with each letter reproduced in exact detail and with footnotes to explain even the obvious. Instead he has fitted the letters into a skeleton narrative, bridging gaps between them and supplying enough information and background to make each intelligible. The result is a work that must rank among the minor classics that describe and picture the Old West. It is also a delightful book to read, as warm and vivid as it is rich in information. The world of scholarship, no less than the world of art, must pay tribute to Alfred Sully for writing and painting as he did, and to Langdon Sully for sharing his ancestor's talents with the wider world.

Ray Allen Billington
THE HUNTINGTON LIBRARY

Preface

About forty years ago my mother gave me two large crates containing the letters and personal papers of my grandfather, Gen. Alfred Sully, and suggested that I sort them out, collate them, and make typewritten copies of each one. This was no small task. A student at Columbia College, I had to do this with what little time I could spare from my studies and my jobs. Alfred's handwriting was not always the most legible due to the conditions under which he frequently had to write. Furthermore, I had to work with a battered old typewriter that was a sometime thing. The part-time project took the better part of three years.

There were some 350 letters: eighty from the pre-California period, and a like number covering his time in California; twenty from the period between his California years and the Civil War; about sixty written during the Civil War; and about a hundred covering the period from the end of the Civil War until his death. In addition, there were a great many newspaper clippings, official reports, and documents issued by the War Department. All of this material is now on loan to the Henry E. Huntington Library in San Marino, California, and is available for research.

In putting the book together I drew heavily on the California and Civil War letters. But there are few letters covering the period of his frontier duty in Minnesota and the Dakotas, and few letters covering his campaign against the Sioux and the Cheyennes in 1863, 1864, and 1865. For these periods I had to go back to government records, newspaper accounts, and the research done by other authors whose names and titles appear in the bibliography.

Most of Sully's letters were written to his sister Blanche and shared with his family. Alfred was such a finished writer that I have not had the temerity to edit what he wrote. The quotations as shown in this book are Alfred Sully's words almost verbatim, even to errors of spelling or punctuation. Instead what I have done has been to extract enough of his writing to provide a continuous narrative by supplementing this with other documented material. I say "almost verbatim" in case I have made a few undetected errors.

First credit for this book must be given to Alfred Sully for writing such vivid letters and for painting such graphic pictures. At the same time credit must be given to my mother who had the foresight to preserve the letters and to keep me at the task.

I am particularly indebted to Dr. Ray Allen Billington of the Huntington Library for his constructive criticism and enthusiastic support. My thanks also go to Ron Tyler of the Amon Carter Museum of Western Art for his encouragement and sound suggestions on the text.

Books given to me by Charles W. Lake, Jr., of the Lakeside Press proved to be a valuable research source.

No book dealing with history could possibly be written without the help of interested research librarians, and in this I was given generous time and assistance by the librarians at the Huntington Library; the National Archives; the United States Military Academy; the Historical Societies in North Dakota, South Dakota (Janice Fleming), Oregon, and Minnesota (Donald Empson), as well as the public libraries in the California cities of Carlsbad, Oceanside, San Diego, Santa Barbara, and Monterey. Julie Almack of the Carlsbad City Library was particularly helpful in turning up that certain book when I needed it and could not locate it myself. Fred Hastert of the Oceanside Public Library also contributed a great deal.

Harry Downie, curator of the Mission San Carlos Borromeo at Carmel, shared his incredibly extensive knowledge of the mission period. Mrs. Sylvia Griffiths at the Santa Barbara Historical Society and Russell Ruiz of Santa Barbara were also most helpful, as was Father Maynard Geiger, O.F.M., head of the Mission Archives located in that city.

Joseph Vogelius, who is also a grandson of Alfred Sully, and his wife Trisket took a deep and continuing interest in the project, assembling pictures from his four sisters who live near his home in Mendham, New Jersey. Mr. Vogelius located the sketchbooks that Alfred carried with him most of the time and shipped a great number of Alfred's pictures to me for photographing. In this connection it is interesting to note that although some of Alfred's sketches, paintings, and watercolors are owned by museums, the bulk of about 100 of them assembled for this project remain in the hands of his grandchildren. My sister Ruth Sully provided much material.

Alfred's great-granddaughter Mrs. Ciro Suganieli also devoted much time in research for the book. There are many others who helped, and if I have failed to acknowledge their contribution the omission is inadvertent.

Finally I am grateful to my wife who traveled with me to the places where Alfred lived in California, helping me to gather information firsthand, and who aided me with research and criticism as the book developed.

Langdon Sully

Chapter One

Orders to California

WHEN HE SAILED from New York for California, Alfred Sully had visions of a long, pleasant cruise with few military responsibilities. As regimental quartermaster, he had made sure that his six-month supplies of impedimenta were all safely stored and secured against foul weather, and all he had to do was to inspect them from time to time to make sure that they remained so and that there was no pilfering.

He pictured himself in California in the generous quarters befitting his rank of first lieutenant in the United States Army, with a servant or two and with light duty. The towns would be picturesque enough to sketch—all adobe and red tile; beautiful girls dressed in bright colors would be plentiful. There would be dancing every night; soulful guitars would strum against a background of soft murmuring waters falling from courtyard fountains.

The young officer who stood dreaming of the pleasures awaiting him in California was by nature and by family background a romantic and an idealist. Alfred was a self-taught artist who had begun to draw at the age of six and was turning out creditable watercolors of Philadelphia, where he lived, by the time he was

Portrait of Alfred Sully as a young man at West Point, painted by his father, Thomas Sully.

thirteen. He received little or no encouragement in these artistic endeavors from his father, although Thomas Sully was one of the foremost artists of his time. A painter of portraits, he had depicted more than twenty-four hundred of the most famous people of his day, including presidents, statesmen, actors, the military, the wealthy, and people destined to be famous. Alfred, on the other hand, liked to paint the scene around him—landscapes, seascapes, animals, and Indians.

There was no common bond between father and son regarding their artistic efforts, but both felt that Alfred would best utilize his talents as a draftsman and an engineer, for he had a unique interest in things mechanical. Through his father's connections, he was able to obtain an appointment to West Point in 1837.

As the time approached to leave for the military academy, he dreaded the separation from his family. Besides his mother and father, Alfred had a brother and eleven sisters. Closest of all was his sister Blanche, six years older than Alfred. Throughout his life she would be his tie to the family; it was through his correspondence with her that he kept in touch. But Alfred's youthful anticipations usually turned out to be wrong. He found that he liked the military academy, and examinations about which he worried for weeks turned out to be simple. The classmates whom he at first regarded as fellow cell-mates soon made him forget his homesickness,[1] and home was not so far away that his sisters could not visit him in relays with boxes of goodies.

One thing he resented was the apparent lack of purpose in sending him out in freezing weather on guard duty to patrol a parade ground that no one would ever invade. He froze in the barracks, too, until he had his quarters changed. He wrote to Blanche, "I have moved my quarters to the arch left of the North Barracks, that is to say the fourth story. I found that it did not exactly agree with me to sleep in such small rooms; with a fire the North Barracks are a great deal better in that respect, for besides having a large room to study in, we have a room to sleep in, and my window commands a fair view of the Hudson, the

19

This is one of the first watercolors Alfred Sully did while he was at the United States Military Academy and perhaps one of the earliest sketches

ever made there. The artistic talent he inherited from his more famous father was to be put to good use.

The quarters provided for officers and their families at West Point were subjects of Alfred Sully's watercolors and sketches.

Crow's Nest, etc." The Crow's Nest, with its broad sweeping view of the Hudson, intrigued him and was the subject of one of the first watercolors Alfred did of West Point.

He was graduated from West Point on July 1, 1841, and before his insignia was even tarnished, he was ordered to Florida to fight in the Seminole Indian conflict. About thirty years prior to this time, the Seminoles had been incited to war against the United States by the British, and although the English had long since backed off, the Americans still had to contend with the Indians.

Alfred welcomed his assignment. He hoped to find glory and possibly a promotion in the battles. But while he did engage in the attack of Hawe Creek Camp on January 25, 1842, his battle was not only with the Indians but with the mosquitoes and other small pests. His outfit spent its time chasing the Seminoles through the hillocks and swamps until it finally wore them out enough to make them surrender. While there were a few skirmishes here and there, it was basically a mopping-up operation and his regiment captured fewer than two hundred Indians to climax its part in the campaign.

Alfred's next combat duty came in the war with Mexico. For nearly five years he had divided his time between garrison duty at Sackett's Harbor, New York, and recruiting service. Now he hoped that Veracruz would bring close contact and hand-to-hand fighting, for his youthful enthusiasm made him overeager for the glory that he expected from combat.

On March 9, 1847, he landed with twelve thousand other men on the beach near the city, and they set about preparing to bombard Veracruz. The terrain between the beach and the walls of the town was rough and sandy; as a result it took almost two weeks to get all of the artillery into place.[2] Batteries of eight-inch guns, mortars, and howitzers were to be supplemented by cannon fire from two steamers and five smaller sailing vessels anchored just offshore. The actual bombardment lasted only four days. By then the town was a complete shambles, and the Mexicans gave up. Alfred's infantry unit had little to do but watch and guard the emplacements against small harassing parties of Mexicans. Although Alfred belittled his role, the army must have attached some significance to the fact that he was in combat and had seen action in the operations against the Indians, for he was promoted to first lieutenant on March 11, 1847, while the siege was still on.

Of the surrender he wrote,

Such a place of destruction I never again wish to witness. The city is built in a very ancient style, great sums having been expended on it, but it has been suffered to go to decay and is the dirtiest city I have ever been in. It is very closely built, having many tall buildings, lofty domes and steeples, and entirely surrounded by a wall and fortifications. In consequence of which our shells and shot have caused dreadful havoc, going

23

Sully's eye for detail and his skill as a draftsman are evidenced in this sketch he did at Veracruz.

through and through the houses and in some places cutting a complete street where before were rows of buildings, and causing great destruction of life, the traces of which you can see in the streets. I am sorry to say that women and children have suffered much from our fire, though they had nobody but themselves to blame for it. General Scott gave them warnings of his intentions, but, Mexican-like, they depended too much on the strength of the place.

The surrender of Veracruz was like something out of an operetta or a musical comedy. Although the Mexicans had had about five hundred civilians and four hundred soldiers killed, they came out of the gates proudly, as if they had just won a great victory. The American troops were drawn up in line of battle before the walls of the town. The gates opened to the sound of horns and the roll of drums, and more than twenty-eight hundred Mexican soldiers in full dress uniform marched out and passed in review before the enemy. Then they halted, wheeled into line, stacked their arms, and marched off. This was the signal for the American detachment designated as the guard for the city to march into Veracruz and hoist the American flag on the different bulwarks. They saluted the flag each time with the Mexicans' own guns.

Alfred commented on the victory:

We certainly got the place very cheap and with only one-fifth of the armament that General Scott and his Engineers thought would be necessary. We have to thank Col. Totten and his Engineers for the masterly manner in which the work was conducted. Had the gallant Old Zach been here he would have made us ram our heads against the walls. The Mexicans expected us to do so and had everything prepared for it so that our loss would have been tremendous.

After Veracruz he was put on guard duty:

I am writing this in an old deserted Mexican apothecary's shop on the Jallapa [sic] Road, my Company being on picket on this road, some 3 or 4 miles from the city (which you know is in our possession) having no other writing material than this Mexican Military Document which I picked up in the Castle of San Juan d'Ulloa and my pencil. When I tell you that I am in an apothecary shop, don't imagine it a place like Fred Brown's. No, it is far from that, being nothing but a thatched cottage with one large window in front serving for door, counter and everything else like this. Now imagine me stretched out on the ccounter with the candle under one of the large broken shop bottles to keep the wind from blowing it out, while on the shelves around me are strewed pill boxes, broken boxes, broken bottles, etc. I feel like poor Nell in the Curiosity Shop. A solitary cat (I suppose one of the household) my only

Alfred always seemed to find the time to record what he saw. He probably did this scene during the proverbial ten-minute break.

companion, with an intolerable stench of calomel, jallop, etc.

There's a small harp in *my shop*. I wish one of you were here to play on it—and a large mahogany bedstead in the back room. I have been looking at it all night with curious eyes, not daring to even go near it for fear of going to sleep. My men are in a sort of barn back of me, making themselves quite comfortable roasting chunks of meat. Happy dogs, all they think about is eating, drinking and sleeping.

From Jalapa, Alfred had gone on toward Mexico City. It was not a forced march, and he had time to sketch the towns they passed. The army was en route to Monterrey, crossing the Rio Sierra and passing through towns like Altamira and Victoria. The war was about over, and before they reached Mexico City, Alfred

Rio Sierra is hard to find today. But it was important enough for Sully to sketch as his forces marched into Mexico after taking Veracruz.

and some other officers were sent back to the United States on recruiting service. After a brief assignment at Jefferson Barracks, Missouri, in 1848, Alfred came to Fort Hamilton, off the tip of Manhattan, where his proximity to New York City allowed him frequent visits to the favorite haunts of a bachelor officer with artistic interests. It was from Fort Hamilton that he boarded the *Iowa* in November 1848 for his five-month voyage to California.

The ship swung to and fro at anchor as the captain waited for a favorable breeze. As he stood on deck, Alfred thought about home, West Point, and the Mexican War. He wistfully recalled Barnum's, St. Paul's, and the Astor House, the New York Gallery of Arts and the fine prints at the American Art-Union. He could savor the drinks at the Gem Saloon on Broadway and the music and beer at the German Winter-Garden on the Bowery. He could almost see them, and he promised himself that he would visit them all again if he should ever get back to New York.

Finally a brisk wind came up, and the ship weighed anchor.

We left Sandy Hook, the guns of the fort firing a farewell salute, with a brisk N'wester, and by night the lights of the Hook could just be made out. All remained on deck till late, but there appeared to be very little disposition on the part of many, particularly the ladies, to be talkative or amusing. Some few had pieces of white cambric to their eyes. I walked the decks till late, smoked, smoked and made many good plans to pass my time both profitably and agreeably both of which I have been unable to do. The wind began to cause the ship to pitch and dance. The sails had to be reefed & in the midst of the confusion I made my escape to my berth. The next morning we were going as if the old gentleman had kicked us on end as the sailors say. Not many showed themselves at the breakfast table, not a single lady I'm sure, but many dismal sounds from weak stomachs were heard from the staterooms, & loud cries for the steward. This weather continued for about 2 weeks, at the end of which, having sailed E. by S., we found ourselves off the coast of Africa & in the trades. Light winds & sunshine brought the ladies and children out of their beds & into their health. Then my troubles, our troubles began. Such children I never saw in my life, nothing but fighting, squalling, crying. We got near the line in the regions of rain. Rained all day for a week, by the buckets full. Every body had to be shut up in a little bit of cabin. The women began to grumble. The children began to fight and squall & the Irish servants began to jaw. It was beyond the bearance of every man but Job, so we, that is the bachelors, got together all the Indian rubber capes, built a sort of tent on the deck & staid there in the rain rather than in the hot nasty cabin. We are altogether too crowded for such a long voyage. The weather is hot. We are all beginning to become a little cross.

He took refuge in his hot little three-by-six-foot cabin and found comfort in his whiskey and "segars." When the water became bad and filled with bugs, the passengers used it sparingly. Not so Alfred. He had a way of killing the bugs before drinking them, although he was sure the temperance people would not approve.

The *Iowa* spent from Christmas to New Year's Day in port at Rio de Janeiro getting fresh supplies and then set sail for Cape Horn. Alfred's next letter described the rest of his long trip:

As we are now about 800 miles out of Valparaiso, our second stopping place, I begin my second letter. Our stay at the port will be as short as possible, just time to fill up with water & fresh provisions. I wrote my last at Rio Janeiro. The Harbor [there] is one of the finest in the world, perfectly land locked, a large basin surrounded by lofty, & to my mind the most picturesque mountains I have ever seen. The town is built on the south side of this basin, about 4 miles from the sea, at the foot of the mountains, on the hills, in the valleys, & in fact all over in spots and clusters—though the largest part it forms a very dirty though interesting looking place;—on the water's edge here are all the stores, markets, palaces & it looks very much like a town in Mexico, only it smells worse, has more fleas, & twice as many niggers. In fact that is one of the most remarkable things about the place; they have a great number of slaves, yet a nigger gentleman is as much of a gentleman as anybody, & in some cases they own nigger slaves. The women are ugly and everything very dirty.

Early in the morning on the first of January we pulled up our mud hook (anchor) & with the assistance of the boats' crews from the frigate (*The Brandywine*) were towed out to sea. I left Rio with some regret, the ladies with a great deal. I had two great objections to it—the smart heat & the fleas. We stood along the coast with a slight breeze, now and then catching up to vessels and passing them, for this ship *Iowa* is quite a fast sailing craft—nothing remarkable happening except the mis-

The fast-sailing ship Iowa *left New York on November 8, 1848, and arrived in Monterey, California, on April 12, 1849. Alfred Sully endured a trip*

punctuated by brawling babies and "jawing" Irish women through the prudent use of whiskey and cigars.

fortune to lose one man overboard. The ship was going so fast he drowned before a boat could reach him. In about two weeks we came to the Falkland Islands. It was our intention of course to have some clearance of them, but head winds drove us on to them, and while we were thinking of going to the outside a calm came and left us within 10 miles of them all day. In the evening, however, a fair wind sent us again on our course, & in a few days we came within sight of Statenland, a small island to the east of Iona del Jugo. Here we were becalmed in sight of the snow hills, & amused ourselves in shooting the sea birds—Albatross, penguins and all the tribes of the South Seas. The wind sprang up the next morning & we tried to get through the Straits between Statenland and the mainland, about 9 miles long and very dangerous. The wind however increased to a gale from the South west, and we were glad to get under the line of Iona del Jugo. That night the wind changed to the North, made sail again, & succeeded in getting clear by next morning. (I mean breakfast time, for it was light from 3 in the morning until 10 at night.) This was Saturday, January 20th. Next day we were in sight of the Horn, but head winds kept us off, and we ran in a zigzag course, going South to nearly 60 degrees. It blew heavy squalls day and night, with hail and rain. However in ten days, by good management, we were around the Horn in good weather again, with no other bad result than a few ladies frightened, several bottles of wine broken in our staterooms, & many things smashed in the pantry—for some of the seas were very near being mountain high. It is now Sunday, the 4th of February, & we are now about 300 or 400 miles from Valparaiso. If this wind holds we will be there day after tomorrow.

We arrived at Valparaiso, Chile, on the afternoon of the 6th February making the passage from Rio Janeiro in the remarkably short period of 36 days. The steamship *Massachusetts* with the 1st Artillery arrived the same day. They left Rio with us. The *Rome* arrived on the 8th. Valparaiso is built on the side of a hill, or hills, facing the open sea; it is not a harbor, nothing but an open roadside—protected from the winds by a Cape. The city at the foot of the hill is well built and paved, but on the side of the high hills are little one story houses, built of sun burnt mud, covered with tiles, with stairs and winding alleys leading from house to house or rather from top to top, to the summit of the hill. These houses of course are filled with the lower orders of society & low enough they are. Just like Mexicans. The ladies are pretty . . . we received a great deal of attention, were much questioned in regards to our service in the Mexican War, & particularly of California and the gold mines. This last topic is all that is spoken of or thought of. Many rebels have arrived here with gold, & all the people are wild with the gold fever. You have no doubt by this time heard wonderful accounts of the gold regions through the papers—they may appear to you, as they did to me, exaggerated and not to be believed, but from all that I can learn from conversing with persons and officers just from there your accounts cannot be more wonderful or monstrous than what I have heard; so believe them all, and believe moreover that you have not heard but half. Sailors, soldiers, men, women & children are all rushing by the thousands after gold. And what is more they all find it at a rate on an average of $15 a day. There is one lump here in town of solid gold, picked up, valued at $400. Labor of all kind has stopped, ships laid up for want of a crew, officers left without a soldier to command—an officer of the U.S. Ship *Lexington* just arrived from there told me the last time he saw Col. Mason, the governor of the place, he was cooking his own dinner. Flour sells in San Francisco at $25 the barrel, and at the mines for any price you choose to ask for it. 4,000 people have now left this place for the gold mines. Six vessels are now in the harbor loading with provisions, and many more every day. What we will do I can not yet see. All our men will leave us the moment they put their feet ashore. We will be a regiment without soldiers. The captain of the ship fears he will be left without a sailor to unload the ship. I am thankful I have nobody but myself. The ladies and children are much to be pitied. What they will do I can't see. The pay of a captain in the army[3] will not even pay the hire of a servant maid so they will have to cook, wash, etc., for themselves and thank God they have something to eat. I have laid out my course. I will dispose of all of my surplus baggage, to save it from being stolen from me, which I can do at a great profit, and if the worst comes to the worst, with my rifle and a few friends push across the mountain, home. As yet everything is uncertain. We will hope for the best. Instead of going to San Francisco, where all the gold fever, or as they call it yellar fever, is raging, we go to Monterey . . . and I suppose it will be necessary to make a compromise with the men, giving them at a time permission to go to gold digging, and thereby keep up a semblance of military discipline until fever shall pass away, or government do something for us.

It would not be long before Alfred himself fell victim to this same fever.

It is not clear whether the *Iowa* changed its destination from San Francisco to Monterey because the rush to the mines had left so many ships deserted in San Francisco, which was closer to the diggings, or because the military government of the United States had been established in the old Mexican capital of Monterrey.

THE UNITED STATES had acquired California as a result of the Mexican War in February 1848. Ever since Mexico had taken over control of the province from Spain in 1822, conditions in California had been chaotic—politically, economically, and sociologically. During the Mexican years there were two principal factions in California, and they were constantly at odds with each other.

One faction was the church and its missions with extensive landholdings up and down the coast from San Diego to San Francisco.[4] The other was made up of the presidio-pueblo com-

plexes in the principal towns, composed of the military government and the civilian government, and populated by Spaniards,
Mexicans, and Indians. The wealth here was concentrated in the
hands of a few families—the de la Guerras, Carrillos, Castros,
Picos, Bandinis, Sepulvedas, Lugos, Ortegas, and Noriegas—the
gente de razon, or aristocracy, who had received land grants from
the king of Spain. As an officer in the United States Army, Sully
would eventually be acceptable to these people, and the de la
Guerras, Noriegas, and Jimenos in particular would play an important part in his life in California. The Church was jealous of
these rancheros who had land grants, but at the same time recognized their power.

Mexico destroyed the internal structure of California in less
than two decades.[5] First the missions were secularized. All of the
land was taken away from them; their agricultural and manufac-
turing operations were no longer pursued, and the once powerful
friars were left with no more responsibility than to run their
churches as parish priests. The mission buildings themselves
were permitted to fall into ruins, and their once lush fields were
left uncultivated.

Next, the number of land grants was increased from about
twenty to almost six hundred in less than twenty years. This
weakened the position of the purebred Spanish ranchero.

Communication between the Mexican capital and the province
was virtually nil. There were no police force, no adequate army,
and no navy; there were no mail, no courts, no jails, no justice,
and no banks.[6] The Mexicans fleeced the treasury and finally in
February 1845, were forced to flee the country, leaving behind a
governor, Don Pío Pico, and a commandante general, Don José
Castro, who constantly opposed each other when they were not
busy fighting Mexicans or Indians.

Meanwhile, more than a thousand Americans, mostly of questionable repute, had come into California over the mountains or
from ships which they had deserted; they now wanted freedom
from rule by Mexico or any other foreign power.[7] Several powers

had their covetous eyes on California in the 1840s. Russia had been engaged in the sea otter trade up and down the coast since shortly after the turn of the century and had established a base on the Pacific; France was interested in making the area a French protectorate; England had been negotiating with Mexico for its purchase; and the United States wanted the real estate any way it could get it, in keeping with its policy of Manifest Destiny. On October 20, 1842, Commo. Thomas ap Catesby Jones had seized Monterey, the capital, under the mistaken belief that the United States was at war with Mexico;[8] when he learned that his action was premature, he apologized and gave it back to the Mexicans. The United States tried peaceful means of annexing California as a territory through its consul in Monterey, Thomas O. Larkin, a successful businessman. It also sent Col. John C. Frémont to explore the situation, but Gen. José Castro branded him a spy and told him to leave the country.

The outbreak of the Mexican War brought the situation to a head. Commo. John D. Sloat took over Monterey on July 7, 1846.[9] The United States also took possession of Los Angeles, San Diego, and San Francisco after only minor skirmishes with the Californians, who really did not care who won as long as some power established a stable government.

Before the *Iowa* reached Monterey, Alfred heard talk that the stable government to be set up there was to be initially a military government and that he was to be the quartermaster and collector of customs of "this important dependency of the United States." He did become quartermaster, but not collector of customs. However, all monies collected were turned over to him; out of them he paid necessary government expenses, transmitting any balance on hand to Washington whenever the government ordered him to do so. He was required to turn in a monthly report on financial conditions.

Although the United States acquired California by right of conquest, the government paid Mexico $15,000,000 for the present states of California, Nevada, Utah, Arizona, and approximately half of Colorado and New Mexico—in all about 918,000 square miles. In addition, the United States assumed claims of Americans against Mexico in the amount of $3,500,000.

At about the time the treaty of peace was signed with Mexico, gold was discovered near Sacramento. The news was quick to spread around the world and within a year, foreigners had already been to California, made their fortunes, and returned home. With the discovery of gold, the sleepy little towns grew so fast that the population of California jumped from less than 10,000 to more than 250,000 by 1852. San Francisco, nearest port to the gold fields, suffered a growth from 800 to 25,000 in two years. These were rowdies and fortune hunters, gamblers and prostitutes, saloonkeepers, speculators, adventurers, and opportunists, with just enough literate merchants and professional people among them to provide the basis for San Francisco's development as a center of culture once the gold fever had died down. The emigrants came mostly from Chile, Australia, Mexico, and the eastern part of the United States.

In the few months he had been at sea, Alfred Sully became apprehensive about what he might find in California. As the *Iowa* rounded Point Pinos, the Monterey he saw was much as he had imagined it would be. The harbor was U-shaped, with high, sandy cliffs on one side and a gently sloping beach at the base of the U. Tall pines topped the hills in the background, and between the hills and the beach was the town. Here were the white adobe houses and red tiled roofs he had expected to find, scattered about the hillside and sparkling in the sunshine. There was a fort with an American flag flying in the breeze, a customs house at the water's edge, and a new two-story building beside it. Alfred was to be the quartermaster of the province and this building was to be his headquarters and commissary.[10] It was all much as he had pictured it. The only indication that everything was not normal was the presence of a few weathered ships that were obviously deserted riding idly at anchor in the bay.

After a few days ashore Alfred found that Monterey was far

When Alfred arrived in Monterey, he lived in the customshouse with the governor, the secretary of state, and the adjutant general.

from the idyllic town he had imagined. He could see all that he wanted to see in a few hours. The purebred Spanish were stand-offish; the Mexicans and Indians were shiftless. Most of the able-bodied men had left the town and gone off to the gold fields. There were no eating or drinking places, and the dancing señoritas and soulful guitars he had imagined as he left New York were only that—imagination. As the weeks passed, he became completely disenchanted, and in time he was to become downright bored.

He also found that labor was impossible to come by.

I would rather be a mechanic in the States than a gentleman here where every loafer has more money and can make more money than you.

I went to a blacksmith the other day with Major Rucker of the

38

Dragoons who was travelling to the North and his horse was very much in want of shoes. I asked him to shoe him. "No sir. I don't wish to do dirty work and I don't like it. Besides I drank too much wine at dinner yesterday and I don't feel quite well. But if you can't do without shoes I will make them for you and you can put them on yourself."

A gentleman the other day arrived from San Francisco, offered a loafer on the wharf $4.00 to carry his trunk. His reply was, "Stranger, I'll give you two ounces ($30) if you'll carry it up yourself. I would like to see you carry that darned thing with your kid gloves." My stable boys I have to pay $100 a month and even then have to do most of the work myself. At this moment I am scratching myself from the effect of flea bites, having been most of the day in the stable yard helping to harness wild mules to wagons—I black my own boots, get my own water, and when my room looks very dirty and I feel uncomfortable in consequence I brush it out. You can imagine how often that is. . . .

Got some wood this morning. Not dear, only six dollars a cord, but it never saw an axe. I have got the top of a tree in the fire. The trunk and branches are on the floor, reach about the middle of the room. As fast as it burns off we push it further in. . . .

The ships that brought us here have lost part of their crews and will lose them all no doubt before they can be unloaded. Some have been shot while deserting, but that don't stop others from trying the same game. The Company of Artillery here holds on its muster rolls 20 men. Of this 20, 6 are here and the rest at the mines. These stay only because they are promised to be let off as soon as the others come back. Our men have mostly left us. A party of 30 started off together. The officers armed themselves, mounted and brought them back.[11] They are now serving out their time in irons. So out of a company of 70 we have but 20 left for duty. Some have furloughs with permission to dig. . . .

It is thought, and I think so too, that by sending the main body of troops to the mines, allowing them to dig for themselves, we may be able to keep up some semblance of military order. I will therefor most probably by the time this reaches you, be up in the region of digging. I have made, or am making all of my arrangements to go, selling off all my luxuries, i.e., extra shirts and the like, & putting myself in camp trim. You never saw anything like the price of things in this country. Provisions enormous. 50 cents apiece for eggs. Labor the same, 10 dollars a day for a man. But articles of clothing and the like cheaper than in New York, that is some articles, the market being overstocked by the immense number of refills arriving daily. Everybody is speculating in land in San Francisco & it is about as dear as in Philadelphia.

The speculators and those who sell goods make all the money. Many of those who send out goods will be ruined, for it costs more to land their goods than they are worth. Ships are glad to sell their cargos below their original cost to get rid of them and get off, for a sailor cannot be obtained for any price.

If you hear of anybody wanting to make money, tell them to charter a ship, load her with frame houses ready to set up, and have her out here before winter sets in. I'll warrant they will more than double their money, for where people are to live that are coming here is more than I can say. I don't believe there will be trees enough in the country to build them houses.

Most of the people were too busy digging gold to cultivate the ground; as a result food was scarce except at the big ranchos, which had Indian servants. Alfred lived from hand to mouth. For a while he lived off the commissary. Wherever he smelled a dinner cooking, he would "ring in" in hopes of being invited to stay. Finally, he teamed up with a Dr. King and Lt. Nelson H. Davis,[12] and they rented a house that cost a hundred dollars a month and for which, according to Alfred, they would have had to pay a thousand in San Francisco. They hired a cook and "lived well," the standard bill of fare being coffee, ham, flapjacks, and molasses for breakfast; beef, rice, tea, coffee, ham, and flapjacks for dinner; and for lunch and supper whiskey and pipes.

This arrangement broke up when the cook ran off to the mines. Alfred was then fortunate enough to be introduced to Doña Angustias Jimeno, the daughter of Don José de la Guerra, one of the most powerful men in California. The doña was a beautiful, cultured woman whose many generosities endeared her to the entire population. Alfred could not praise her too much in his letters to Blanche:

> When she found that it was impossible for the officers here to mess for themselves she offered them her house, for which her Spanish pride would not allow her to accept money. So the officers to pay her were obliged to make her presents. These officers have now all been ordered away except for Capt. Halleck (whom you may have remembered at West Point).[13] It was through his influence I got my present situation. She (the Doña) is a tall, majestic looking woman, about 30 or 35, remarkably handsome, very clear complexion, red cheeks, black hair, very agreeable, very good natured and very smart. In fact she is a well read woman and would grace any society. Her oldest child is a daughter about 15 or 16 years old. Doña Manuela, remarkably pretty and gay, dances and sings and plays the guitar and is, like all Spanish girls, monstrous fond of a flirtation. I fear she finds this rather a hard job with me, for my bad Spanish sets her a laughing. However that don't prevent me from having a very agreeable time of it, for she has a good figure, a good foot and ankle, small hand, brilliant black eyes, white teeth, red cheeks and as lively as a cricket. The Don is a very polite Spaniard, is seldom at home. Most of his time is spent at his ranch.
>
> I have been doing little or nothing, waiting here to start for Benicia, and though my time has been idly, it has not been unprofitably spent. I have become quite a native. Can live on tortillas and frijoles, smoke cigarettes through my nose, speak

Alfred made many sketches of Manuela but was
never satisfied with any of them.

Spanish (though d—ish bad) and somewhat initiated into the mysteries of the Spanish Doñas, waltzes and Polkas. So that's not so bad.

About three weeks ago Don Manuel, the husband, went off to his rancho. There being no male in the house, Me Madre (that is the name she calls herself) though she is rather young and handsome to have so old a boy as me, requested me to make her house my home.[14] So I have shifted my quarters from the barracks to two nicely furnished rooms and pleasant company. The manners of the Spanish of the higher class are very much the same as a Southern planter; in place of Negroes they have Indians for servants, and in this house plenty of them. They are generally to strangers somewhat cold in their manners, yet very hospitable. But once acquainted all restraint is thrown off.

Alfred was bored with his duty at Monterey and unhappy at the inequity of a situation where everyone was in a position to make money except the army officers. He asked for a leave to dig gold; request denied. He was offered a business deal on which he said he could have netted five thousand dollars in two months; again his request for a leave was denied. But he had to supplement his income somehow in order to live.

The only thing I have made money on is horse flesh. I first owned a large California yellow horse, but as he had a habit of putting his head down and jumping like a rabbit, thereby succeeding in letting me down in not the most gentle manner possible, I was glad to sell him for what I gave. The next was an iron gray pony who always had a fight when you put his bridle on. So I sold him for $50 more than I gave. My next was a beautiful brown American horse which I bought from a Dragoon Officer; but as a gentleman offered me $250 more than I gave for him I thought it best to sell him.[15] I now own a large American light gray, just enough of the devil in him to make him interesting to ride on without being dangerous.

Alfred's letters to Blanche showed that he was impressed by such aspects of California as the size of families, the speed with which towns sprang up, and the fact that the makeshift system of law and order somehow worked:

I just returned the other day from a visit to a silver mine, not now in operation. It is on the ranch of an Englishman who has lived in this town some thirty years, is married to a Spanish lady who has just presented him with his 21st child. It is a remarkable thing about these Californians, their large families. They generally marry when they are 12 to 16 years old and have an addition to the family every year until they are fifty. Thank God they don't all live or the country would not be large enough to hold them all.

43

The officers give wonderful accounts of things at the Placers. Towns and cities springing up in every direction and everything showing the enterprise of the Yankee nation. At a town, I believe Sacramento, they gave the General (General Bennett Riley, the Military Governor) a dinner. Two days before the dinner the lumber for the house in which they dined was not yet purchased; and the dinner that morning was aboard a vessel in the river just arrived from New York. "Go ahead" is the word. Many making fortunes but many will have to smash.

The Convention of Delegates elected by the people by the order of Governor Riley for the purpose of forming a State Constitution will meet here the first of next month [September 1849] and praying to be admitted as a State.[16] Then I hope we will have something like law and order. At present the only law is the good sense of the better proportion of the inhabitants. In every encampment of the diggers they have a man who with a jury of the inhabitants tries all misdemeanors, and there is no prison or men to guard the prisoners, they either punish by the lash or by the cord around the neck.

He attributed most of the crimes to the fact that a great number of mining companies, principally from Sonora in northern Mexico and from South America, were filling the country with "many thousands of worthless cutthroats," and he predicted that the army would soon be given the order to drive these people from United States territory at bayonet point. The miners, however, did not wait for military intervention but drove all Spanish-speaking prospectors out of the country themselves.

After about five months of boring duty at Monterey, Alfred was ordered away on temporary duty to Benicia, a naval and military station situated on the northern tip of San Francisco Bay, about fifty miles from the city. His only regret at leaving was having to say goodbye to Doña Angustias and her family.

44

Chapter Two

Barracks by the Bay

NORMALLY ALFRED TRAVELED ABOUT thirty-five miles a day on horseback; when he was in a hurry, he could make as much as sixty-five miles a day. On the trip to Benicia, however, he had with him wagons drawn by unbroken mules. He had sent these on ahead, but by the time he caught up with them, the mules had kicked their traces, so he decided to stay with them. On the second day out, after crossing prairies where there was nothing to see but grass and sky and large herds of wild cattle, and after easing the wagons through an almost impassable mountain pass, he reached the rancho of Don Manuel, husband of Doña Angustias. The rancho he later described as being as big as the state of Rhode Island; the house, situated beside a river, was much like a southern plantation back in the States but had small Indian, instead of Negro, huts around it.

From Benicia he wrote to Blanche,

We found the Don superintending the killing of his cattle for hides and tallow. The bones and meat were all put into large kettles and boiled, the grease skimmed off and the meat thrown

45

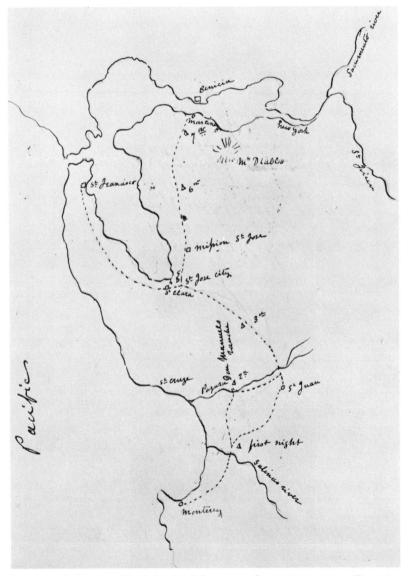

The detailed map Alfred drew of the route from Monterey to Benicia could be used to advantage even today.

away to feed the buzzards. What a waste. He was delighted to see us, turned out all he had in the house and a good bed apiece in the bargain. Next morning after paying him six dollars a bushel for his barley (the price of the country) he started the wagons with an Indian to guide them through the mountains to the main road and we started ourselves to overtake them. . . . We passed through a beautiful country, a broad, rich valley reaching some 30 or 40 miles with mountains on both sides.

The next day we reached San Jose, a thriving little town built up since the gold times, principally by Americans and I should think containing some 3,000 or 4,000 inhabitants. Mostly built of tents and wood. Having some business here I halted on the edge of town. Spent most of the next day there. We were lucky enough in obtaining a Chilean who wanted to go North and volunteered to cook for us on the journey. I suppose I took a particular fancy to him as he had mostly the same name as the young lady at whose home I lived, and he moreover played on the guitar the same Spanish airs that she used to play for me on the bright moonlight evenings.

The next day we rode out on a beautiful road ditched and lined on both sides with willow trees (the work of the priests in olden times) to the mission house of Santa Clara, a distance of three miles. Like all other missions in the country, a long line of low buildings enclosing a square, with a large church in one corner, surmounted by a cupola filled with bells. The roofs are all covered with red tiles. What a happy set of devils those priests must have been in olden times. They had the whole control of the country. Every thirty miles along the coast their large mission houses taking thousands of acres. The Indians were their slaves and their will the law. Yet I have been told by old inhabitants the country never was in a happier state. They never abused their power, were hospitable and kind to all, particularly so to strangers. The Mexican Government became jealous of them, drove them out of the country. Since then their missions have been going to decay. Few of them are left in anything like their former glory.[1]

Next day left the Monterey and San Francisco Road, branched off to the east side of the Bay. Passed through the Mission of San Jose, fifteen miles from the town, and passed on the road some 500 or 600 Sonorans on their way home to Mexico, driven out of the mines by the Yankees. They looked very much disgusted. Few would even have good morning with you. Some drew their pistols and passed us with their fingers on the triggers, looking as black as a thundercloud. Fearing that they might take a notion to something in the wagons I ordered a halt until they were some distance behind. I believe they were more frightened of us than we were of them.

We camped at a beautiful spot that night in sight of Mount Diablo, the highest peak in the coast range. All around us were the snow berries growing wild. We might have reached the town of Martinez opposite Benicia the next day, but as we would be too late for the ferryboat & they say the mosquitoes are the devil there we thought it would be better to stop at a good place 8 miles from there.

That night Alfred almost lost his horse, his most prized possession. It was a large American bay named Dick, which formerly belonged to a sergeant in the dragoons. "A very spirited animal," Alfred described him, "yet one of the most sagacious fellows I ever saw." In the middle of the night, he heard a great snorting and kicking, and found that Dick had gotten his rope tied around his legs so that his nose and forefeet were all tied together. His kicking threatened to break his leg. When Alfred spoke to him and told him to lie down, he did, holding up one foot and then the other to have them untied. Dick obediently made no attempt to move. "I expect Mother would fall in love with him if she was here," Alfred wrote. "He will follow you about like a dog, come into your tent and help himself to anything he likes."[2]

Sully found Benicia a dreary and desolate place, without a tree, shrub, or blade of grass within five miles. The nearest wood was

Sully described the Santa Barbara home of Don Jose de la Guerra as "as antique a looking pile as you wish to see."

miles away, and water, even for cultivation, was two miles from the outpost. The wind blew across the barren land night and day, filling everything with dust. The government had just built a frame barracks designed for one company of soldiers but had placed in it two companies, the band, the hospital, and the administrative headquarters. For each married officer, the army had built a one-story frame house, thirty by twenty feet. The unmarried officers had to find accommodations wherever they could.

"In the opinion of everybody," he wrote, "[this is] the meanest, most uncomfortable place in California. You may ask perhaps why we are sent here. It is known that Commander Jones has lots in the place and it is pretty well known that some officer or officers of the army have them also. They hope that by spending government funds here they may enrich their own pockets and maybe they will succeed in it, in spite of all that is against them.

In the meantime we have to suffer, paying a mess bill of 60 dollars a month and then living in dirt on soldier's rations."

Alfred lived in a tent until the rains washed it away. Then he moved into the hulk of the deserted store ship *Julia* which he found infested with rats, roaches, and fleas. He had to walk half a mile in mud up to his boot tops in order to get to his meals. So he took aboard the sergeant and his wife, who acted as cook and housekeeper.

Alfred had to take wagon teams almost forty miles to lay in the winter's supply of wood for the garrison, since there was nothing closer that would burn. For a time, the station at Benicia lived on quartermaster stores—pork and beans. Rations and supplies were stored on the ground under old, rotted canvas, and the food became inedible. With a lack of good water, meat, and fresh vegetables, scurvy broke out and affected all of the men. Most of them were covered with sores from infected flea bites. Encouraged one day by the appearance of "millions" of wild geese, Alfred sent out a detail of men to bring in as many as they could for at least one or two meals; but he could not go himself, because the sores on his legs made it impossible for him to walk any great distance.

Alfred led an inactive life in Benicia. "I ran down an antelope the other day on horseback but as old Dick is not a Californian and not used to such sports he objected to my firing a pistol near his ear and made me miss. I believe that has been the extent of my sportsmanship since I have been here." Morale became low; even the officers discarded their uniforms. "I have adopted the costume of a woodsman: moccasins, leather legs, hunting shirts and bowie knives. I fear I shall become so rough and unpolished in this country that when I come to the States, if I ever do go into civilization, I shall be a disgrace to the family."

He traveled to Napa and Sonoma in search of a food supply for the garrison, but had no success. He noted that farmers were coming in fast and settling on all the rivers and creeks, "the only places where some good farms are to be found. Next year this will be quite a respectable country to live in. At present it is far from being so."

The food situation grew worse as each day passed. In desperation, Alfred hitched up his wagon teams and headed for Bodega, a small seacoast town about seventy miles away where he was told that he could get fresh vegetables.

Started at ten, my wagons having started at sunrise, reached Sonoma that night. Started the next morning on an unknown road and before going 15 miles got into the mountains and into a rainstorm. Having nothing on but a buckskin shirt and some leggins, the water soaked through like a sieve and wet me to the skin. Luckily I had provided myself with a bottle of whiskey or I should have perished from the cold. I got up in the mountains, a most dreary road, nothing but bare hills covered with dead grass, and a few wild cattle and deer—the rain and mist pelting in my face until I reached the top of a high mountain. Here I took a cattle path in the direction I should go and, directing the wagons to follow, put spurs to Dick determined to find shelter for the night.

I know of no more unpleasant situation for a man to be placed in than to be up in the mountains, without knowing where you are, wet, nothing to eat, and a fair prospect of staying out all night. "Go ahead, old Dick, we must come to someplace before too long." I rode along till night came on when suddenly coming to a steep declivity, where the rains had made the road more dangerous than romantic, I had to rein in my horse. I heard the distant roaring of the seashore. The fog cleared away. The moon shone out, and in the valley below at a distance of two or three miles I saw the white houses of a rancho.

I soon came into the famous Red Wood forests of the country, for the first time. . . . These forests grow in the richest valleys of the country; they look something like a cypress, between a cypress and a pine, very straight and very tall, at least 200 or 300 feet, and 6 feet in bulk; with no undergrowth, the moon shining through and the hooting of owls, I never saw a more dismal scene. I kept my holsters open, and my horse well in hand, expecting at every moment to meet a grizzly bear or some such varmint. But luckily I heard nothing but the dripping of water from the leaves, and the splashing of my horse's feet in the mud, and an occasional snort as he would spy a stump somewhat blacker than the rest. I was not sorry when my arrival at the rancho was announced by the barking of a dozen dogs, the useful appendages to a Californian house, and the *buenas noches* of the Don who came to receive me.

I found the house a true Californian or Mexican house —no comforts, no fire; the women, the Don's wife and two daughters who were by the way very pretty girls, sitting around the supper table wrapped in their rebosas. However they were very kind. The girls ran off, cooked some warm beef and peppers which, with a hot cup of bad coffee, made me feel somewhat comfortable. I found that I had taken the wrong road, or rather direction—for there was no road—and had struck Bodega Valley 6 miles above the place where I wanted to go. I lost nothing in the end by it, for they had the very thing I was after— fresh vegetables.

My wagons came in some hours later, much to the surprise of the ranchero who had no idea they could travel over such a road; it certainly was bad for a night travel. After drying myself before the teamsters' fire, I turned in on the floor to sleep; but, tired as I was, that was a thing not to be had. The fleas gave me fits, and with these and the grunting of two or three Indian girls who had turned in sans ceremony in the same room, I was glad to find a bed in one of the wagons.

The next morning I loaded up the wagons and started them ahead. Don José and his family were also going into Sonoma to attend a church festival, All Saints Day I believe, and wanted me to ride with them. We did not get started until 12, for the Senoritas like all of their sex must keep everybody waiting until their toilet pleases them. As I had shown some attention to one of the prettiest of the party, I was bound to be her gallant for the occasion, but I found I had made a bad bargain, for she was the very devil on horseback, led me a devil of a chase up hills and down valleys. She would go at a full gallop down the steepest hills. A Californian horse is used to this. I have seen them gather their legs and slide down a hill like a goat, but I was afraid that my American horse would stumble, but I was bound to keep up for the honor of my country and the army. She had the impudence to say to me *"El Señor esta bueno Californ-ian."* I believe she did it only in hopes of bluffing me off, devil take her; I like to have spoiled my horse with her mischief.

We reached Sonoma—35 miles—in a very little over five hours. I concluded to rest my horse next day till the wagons got up and then started and reached Benicia at dinner time, in a rain storm; since which time it has been raining without stopping more than a few hours to blow like all out doors.

Water is scarce except in the present rainy season, when it is flooded and perfectly impassable for anything on wheels. Very profitable crops are raised if planted in season, and from December to May the ground is covered with verdure. But after that it is dry, dead, dusty & dreary like a great desert. It is true it has heretofore been in the hands of a lazy improvident nation, who only care for a mud house, enough wood to cook a few beans & beef, & enough ground to produce them, letting their cattle and horses roam about over miles and miles of land, living in good condition when the grass is green, & the best way they can, or die, when there is none. Now that the country is filling with Yankees who will be obliged to do something besides looking for gold, ingenuity & enterprise may, & no doubt will, do wonders for the country. California is a country of contraries, even to the wild game; when it is a good season for hunting it is out of season for killing. Now that the country is knee deep in mud and mire, the plains are actually white with wild geese & the sides of the hills at a distance look as if they were covered with snows.

Whenever he could, Alfred broke the dreary, wet or dusty monotony of Benicia and found some excuse to visit San Francisco. It was September 1849, and San Francisco was getting to be a fair-sized city, though most of the houses were crudely built of boards and canvas, with everybody striving to erect some little shanty for shelter. Whole streets were being built in less than a week. Though some people were already starting to build more substantial houses, the tent cities were for transients—people arriving by ship every day, expecting to make fortunes overnight. Those who did not make it had a hard time booking passage home; all tickets were sold out ahead of time, and the ships' captains were so independent they would not even wait for the mail. Ships cleared $150,000 a trip; captains were paid $500 a month, and a seaman made as much as an army officer.

Business was wild, and the streets were crowded with goods, carts, merchants, and laborers, all seeking ways to make a fast dollar. Alfred found that the only people getting rich were the gamblers. "I have never seen anything like it and I have seen a good deal of gambling in my day. In the open streets night and day they are at it. Every other tent is a gambling shop, drinking shop or store. The most singular thing is that few quarrels take place. I can only attribute that to the fact that everybody is armed and they know very well that an outbreak would be no boy's play."

Prices were still beyond his belief. His boots could not have been bought for a hundred dollars. (He felt they were worth it, however, when he watched a mule hitched to a cart sink in mire over his head and die, while people looked on helplessly.) He looked forward to his trips to San Francisco but was always glad to get out because he could not afford to stay there.

At last his life of boredom ended in late 1849 when he was transferred from Benicia back to Monterey.

Chapter Three

Paradise Glimpsed

ALFRED RETURNED TO MONTEREY, little knowing how much the rest of his life would be shaped by the bittersweet experiences of his next two years. He found that the town had changed a great deal in his absence. There were gambling places and drinking halls without number, four hotels, and many restaurants. "When I was here you could not get a dinner for money; now money will buy anything," he wrote to Blanche.

The doña's house had also changed. When Alfred left for Benicia, her parlor had a sanded floor; the woodwork was painted a bright green, and there were a great number of common chairs ranged around the room in a haphazard fashion, with a big table for books, boxes, and knickknacks. Now she had done over the entire house. The woodwork in her parlor was painted white; there was a fine imported carpet on the floor; mahogany chairs and an upholstered sofa put the finishing touches on a room such as might be found in expensive homes in eastern cities.

The house had changed, but the doña had not. Her home was filled with a party of Spaniards who had just returned from the mines and were awaiting the first available steamship to take them home, so Alfred declined her invitation to move into his old quarters. Instead he found a log cabin on a hill, which he shared with Lt. Tredwell Moore.[1] They shared the cost of a servant and led a comfortable existence, one so pleasant that Alfred was sure he would soon be transferred to a less desirable station.

They started a theatre (which still stands in Monterey), where they produced what was said to be the second show in California. Alfred painted the scenery, wrote the play, and was the principal actor. Army officers played all the parts, male and female. "Although the acting was mighty so-soish," Alfred wrote, "it all came off with a great deal of applause and the audience very much gratified, particularly as they had nothing to pay."[2]

He spent his time surveying town lots, for which he was paid from twenty to thirty dollars a day. He began to put aside his money for a trip to Europe by way of China; he thought he could arrange it because the son of Thomas Ewing, secretary of the interior, planned to go with him and was to make the necessary arrangements in Washington. The trip to China, according to his estimates, would cost about $200; from there to England would cost $900. The trip would take him to the Sandwich Islands, Canton, Ceylon, through the Suez Canal to Naples, Rome, Switzerland, Paris, Madrid, Amsterdam, and London. "Rather a pretty trip," he wrote. "It will cost a great deal of money, I know, but I think it will pay well in enjoyment, in studies and improvement, and I know of no better way to spend what I have got." He had about $3,500. He began to study German in preparation for his trip. He had already studied French at West Point; he spoke Spanish, and he felt that with this background another language would come easily to him.

The nights he spent in what he termed "socializing." In spite of the fact that there were reports of new gold discoveries and people had begun to flock again to the gold fields, the military band had been brought back from the diggings. Dances and fandangos were frequent and furious:

The town has received its charter as a city, and in consequence has had elections and speeches for city officers, and then drinking parties and speeches to get the old officers under Mexican laws out of office. Besides which we have had three balls and one picknick or as they call it here, *merienda*. The first was given by the officers of the army, quite a neat little affair and as select as circumstances would permit, about forty ladies and as many gentlemen. The ladies were more American and appeared better dressed than I have yet seen them. Were it not for their bad taste in selecting colors and their rather dark complexion they might pass under home. But then they waltz so well, have such eyes and natural grace, that they rather knock you. My friends were not there. Manuela and Teresa were out at the ranch and the Doña unwell.

The next was given by the Officers of the County of Monterey. Being a political ball of course it was crowded and not quite as select as it might be . . . . Doña Angustias being unwell, it was thought her daughter and two young ladies staying at her house would be prevented from going also, not having anyone to act as the matrona, when much to my astonishment and everyone else's she turned to me. "If my son Don Alfredo will take my daughter to the ball, she can go." So I had the honor to act as father to three of the prettiest belles in the room.

The next ball was given by the officers of the City of Monterey and the picknick by the citizens of Monterey. This last was the most amusing of the whole. The ladies were dressed in their best silks and satins and many of them had put aside the graceful rebosa (I suppose out of compliment to the Americans) and clapped on their heads bonnets, but such horrors. They were all of one sort: pink, blue and white silk with feather to match and put on their heads in all sorts of ways. The elderly women looked like washerwomen and the girls like servant maids, but I suppose they will have to come to it sooner or later and we may as well get used to it, for everything Spanish is fast melting away before the go ahead Yankees.

The word "picknick" shows up quite often when Alfred wrote from California. He loved parties; he loved the ladies; he loved

*the missions, and he loved animals. All of these are brought out in
this scene he painted of his favorite country.*

The party otherwise, barring the horrors, was *muy alegre*. They had plenty to eat, a roast ox, and plenty to drink. They danced and played pussy wants a corner to the dulcet tones of a very drunken brass band, till at last, the liquor beginning to work, the men began to toss each other up in blankets and play leapfrog while the ladies laughed. However it all passed off very well and then wound up by marching into town in procession with the band ahead playing the "Grand March" from *Norma*.

But the California ladies, not thinking that the quantity of provisions was enough or good enough or thinking that the Americans might have a poor opinion of their liberality, got up another affair of this kind last Sunday which was pretty much the same thing, only we had more to eat and more of a variety to eat (I believe they think of nothing else here but eating and dancing; that and their pride will before long make them beggars in their own land). In the evening we had a dance which wound up the gaieties for the month.

Not only was the boredom of Benicia forgotten in the whirl of social activity, but the seasonal changes made Monterey a delight for the artist in Alfred, and the lushness of the countryside allowed him to endure more easily his military duties:

Nothing can exceed the beauty of this country at this season. The whole ground looks like a rich Brussels carpet covered with every variety of flowers, while the cattle and horses are in beautiful condition, are whisking up their tails and enjoying themselves after their long winter's frost. In front is my horse stuffing himself with grass and biting and kicking at any other horse who presumes to come near him. He runs wild in the fields all day and comes home at night to be groomed and fed.

Alfred also developed interests in other kinds of beauty. He revealed to his family that for some time he had been in love with

*Alfred Sully enjoyed many leisure hours at his father-in-law's
California rancho, where living was easy and hospitality gracious.*

the doña's daughter, Manuela. He was thirty years old, and she
was only fifteen. However, fifteen was considered a marriageable
age in Monterey at that time.

He put aside his plans to take a trip around the world. Manuela
had many suitors, and Alfred was afraid he would lose her. He
was also afraid that her parents would object to the marriage,
because the family was one of the oldest, proudest, and richest in
either California or Mexico, and he had nothing to offer but "his
good family background and reputation." Furthermore, he was a
non-Catholic, and her family was very religious.

To his surprise, when he approached Doña Angustias and Don
Manuel, they gave him permission to discuss marriage with
Manuela, thinking she would refuse him. They had planned to
marry her to a wealthy relative. When she accepted Alfred's pro-
posal, her relatives and friends were so horrified at the idea of her

61

*Life was abundant – and wasted. The meat and bones of cattle were boiled,
the grease skimmed off for tallow, and the meat thrown to the buzzards.*

marrying outside of the church, and marrying a poor American to
boot, that Don Manuel had to find a way out to save face.

The father informed me that for the present I must put it off
until they could get the consent of the grandfather and the two
Padre Uncles. But I knew that as soon as they should hear from
them they would order Manuela to be sent to them for safekeeping where she would have been guarded more strictly
than a nun in a convent. Since they had no objections to me but,
as they said, were only in fear of the displeasure of the Doña's
father, I said nothing, but taking the responsibility into my own
hands acted as I did—although I must admit it was not according to Hoyle as far as the family is concerned.

A friend of Alfred's rode to San Francisco and back to get a
dispensation from the bishop for a Catholic to marry a non-
Catholic; he covered the 240-mile round trip in less than six days.

The next thing was to get around the Padre, Father Ramirez, to marry us without the consent of the parents.[3] The next, to find an opportunity. Mrs. Kane, Captain Kane's lady, invited Manuela to her house on Monday the 20th of May.[4] Her Mother allowed her to go with a young gentleman, a young lover of the young lady's and very much in favor of the old lady. Lieutenant Jones dropped into Captain Kane's *by accident*.[5] His duty was to take care of the gentleman lover. The Padre and myself were hid in some bushes behind the house. Mrs. Kane walked the lady into the kitchen. A white flag from the house was our signal to enter and five minutes later we were married.

The old folks are as mad as well can be. I went to see them and was invited never to show my face again. All the old folks are kicking up quite a row; all the young ones think it quite funny. I believe it's the first elopement that's occurred in California.

Apparently the Thomas Sully family back in Philadelphia was not altogether pleased either, for Alfred wrote home:

I know not what it is that makes a mother or sister dislike to see the male portion of their family marry. You seem to have fears that poverty will be my lot. It is true on some accounts an officer should be the last person to marry on account of the uncertainty of their fate. But if you come to that, who is sure in this life. A man in wealth and luxury may by some misfortune . . . be reduced to want, or by some unforeseen accident lose his life and leave his family beggars in the world. Should the worst befall me I have at least, thanks to you, a good education and a good name to begin the world anew like the rest of mankind. I agree with you there are many reasons why I should have remained in a state of single blessedness, but I have seen many more officers married who get along well in this world, and have not in a single instance seen one single at the age of 40 who was not miserable, with his constitution and energies undermined by dissipation.

But his father, Thomas Sully, explained their concern. He wrote in one of his rare letters to his son:

Dear Alfred—

I have never so much regretted my not being rich as at this time, when I desire to help you in your new situation . . . . Certainly I am glad because you are married, but I fear your little wife will find it a hard matter to battle with a life of difficulty, if not of poverty, after the indulgences she has been used to. Tell her that all we have to offer her are affectionate hearts, and a home with us, where she will be cherished as my other children. My dear son, never be betrayed into an unkind word to her; remember what she has given up for your sake. May God bless you both is my fervent prayer.

Your father,
Thomas Sully

In a fit of passionate anger that immediately resulted from Manuela's elopement, her parents kept all of her belongings, including her clothes. The army wives took a great interest in seeing that she was well dressed, partly because she was so much admired by them and partly to shame the parents. In a few months the doña relented to the extent that she sent Manuela's clothes along with some expensive gifts. These included a satin bedcover embroidered with silk and with a heavy fringe, together with lace-bordered linen sheets. Alfred commented that the spread alone must have cost $250, so "they couldn't be too mad," but he added that he slept better on a blanket before a campfire.

He wanted Manuela to go east and spend some time with his family, so that she could learn English and become used to American customs. When she refused to go without him, he requested a five-month leave so that he could take her to Philadelphia. Again his request for a leave was denied.

It was four or five months before the don and doña sent word that they wanted a reconciliation and would send for Alfred and Manuela soon. But Alfred said that their Spanish pride and his Yankee pride made it difficult for either of them to make the first move. The stalemate was broken when the parents learned that Manuela was to have a baby.

The old man, Don Manuel, is delighted, don't fear, to tell everybody that his daughter is again reconciled. She is the first of this generation to be married; being the oldest child and the favorite of her father it is a great thing for him to separate from her. I suppose there will be a strong move on the part of the family and relatives to have me resign my commission and settle down with them. Hints that way have been made, such as giving me a part of his ranch (which is the best by far in the country), building me a house, etc., but I don't think I should be happy out of the Army. I fear I am a confirmed old soldier for the rest of my life. Don Manuel is old and rich and his oldest son (who is now at school in the United States) is but twelve years old.[6] He wants somebody to take charge of his affairs. He has over twenty working hands, 3,000 or 4,000 head of cattle and nine or ten miles of rich land besides another ranch below of thirty miles extent and other properties besides. 400 acres of the land are fenced for cultivation, all the rest occupied by his cattle.

The family is an old Spanish one, the first and wealthiest in the land, and had I married in the house I could have made a good bargain of it as far as money goes.

Manuela's maternal grandfather was "an old Spaniard living at Santa Barbara who rules the Californians like a king on a small scale." His prestige was further enhanced by the fact that his wife was a Carrillo, one of those families who came to California with a land grant from the king of Spain.

Don Manuel finally persuaded Alfred to take a section about two miles square and to start to develop it. Alfred saw an opportunity to make it pay off quickly:

With the want of money, goods are cheaper than in the United States, many things being sold to pay freight. Strange that in a land of gold there should be no money. But of course this cannot last long. There will be a reaction. As soon as merchants at home find this out they will send nothing, and as California in nothing but meat supplies herself, there must be a want until it turns itself to farming. In view of this I have just made arrangements with two men to settle on some land for me. I am about to put up a sawmill and if I can find a good opportunity shall also go in for a flour mill. I went out to survey Don Manuel's rancho, but could not finish my work for the rains. I surveyed one side about 20 miles on the banks of the river, beautiful land of all sorts: hills, plains, woods, rivers and lakes.

Alfred began to settle down. He wondered what it would be like to be a civilian. He bought a carriage for which Manuela insisted on making the curtains and cushions, while he did the carpentry and upholstery; they used it for picnics with their friends. All of the officers had been transferred or sent out to fight Indians who were raiding the ranches and settlements, so he moved into the house formerly occupied by General Riley, the military governor.

It is very large, having five large rooms on a floor with the kitchen back. I had very little trouble moving, not having much to move and plenty of help. The Doña and all her Indians were hard at work and in a day all was fixed. One large room on the right I use as a parlor, the back room as a chamber; on the left my office and back rooms, dining room and a spare chamber. The family cat, dogs, chickens and horse were moved in the night time without much inconvenience. . . . A hen on 13 eggs under the house I transferred, eggs and all being put into a box and she has been setting there since without being a bit wiser.

He had two Indian servants who had decided to stay with Manuela when she eloped, and a Negro servant in addition; the garden produced fresh vegetables. "Quite a change from an old bachelor's room full of the smell of segars and brandy. Lots of company; decidedly more jolly."

When his sawmill was finished he began to work on his flour mill:

I started the last part of my mill about three weeks ago and started off myself with the miller in the carriage. Twenty miles from Monterey, not knowing the road, got stuck in the mud, at which the horses broke the whipple tree; but having several axe handles along this was soon remedied, but could not make the 35 miles that day. Slept that night under a tree, the road being bad. Night dark and horses wild. I was afraid I would break the carriage, if not our necks. Next morning, without supper or breakfast except a pipe, reached the ranch. Don Manuel was there, glad to see me.

After a good breakfast started for the mountains in the Redwoods. We steered by landmarks, no road. I reached with some trouble the top of a mountain where, in the valley below, was the spot fixed on to erect the mill. A deep glen filled with tall red wood trees from 6 to 10 feet in diameter and over 200 or 300 feet high, straight as a plumb and not a leaf for over fifty feet above the ground, that made the woods look like the interior of some solemn Cathedral. In the middle of the glen a mountain torrent came dashing down through the rocks. Most beautiful, but how to get the wagons there?

Don Manuel knew nothing of it, though on his lands. I dismounted and on foot by good fortune found another glen leading into this in which with four days work and half a dozen men we made a good road leading into the place and two miles nearer. Here I have placed the mill and am only waiting part of the machinery which had to be cast in San Francisco to begin operations. I have orders for $2,000 worth of lumber to be paid off in cattle which I shall sell in Sacramento, so I think if I don't make anything it will at least pay for itself. Having put things in motion I returned.

At a river crossing on his way to Monterey, Alfred met a friend who advised him that Manuela had given birth to a baby boy. There was no doctor within thirty miles, and she was attended by her mother and two old women. The doña herself had just had another baby. She was living at Manuela's because "the Bishop has brought here some nuns to make a convent.[7] They are all staying at the Doña's until their convent is fixed so they have at the house twenty-six souls to take care of for nothing. What would you say if unexpected 26 souls would knock at your door some morning for board and lodging? That's hospitality and that's running it on with a vengeance."

For a while Alfred's house was in a delightful state of confusion and uproar. Crowds streamed in and out. Relatives and friends wanted to offer congratulations and to see the baby. The don was proud to show off his grandson at any time of the day or night, and Alfred was left more or less in the background, happy to get what precious time he could alone with Manuela and his son. At her insistence they named the boy Thomas Manuel Sully after his grandparents.

He contemplated the future with reasonable expectation of a full and joyous life as a California don. There would be more children, more servants, more land and cattle, more activity at his mills, and more farming. Alfred was a truly happy man for the first time since he had left home. His wife, though small and delicate, had borne a strong baby son for him and was ecstatic and in good health.

But then there occurred the first in a series of tragic events that were to embitter Alfred and to change his whole outlook on life. The story told in Monterey was that an ex-suitor of Manuela's sent her some poisoned oranges; some said it was poisoned olives. No one said who sent them. But, poisoned or not, she died a violent death soon after eating the fruit.

On April 30, 1851, Alfred wrote home:

You must by this time have received my short letter announcing the death of my Manuela. So sudden, so unexpected was it that I am only just beginning to believe it reality and not a horrible dream. She was well on the 26th, walking about the house. That morning she brought our child into my room and placed it in bed with me, rubbing her little hands together in perfect child-like delight to see me playing with the baby. She wanted to eat an orange that had been sent her but I, thinking I know not why they might be bad, told her no. Her mother who was present thought they would do her no harm; she would however, ask the doctor (one Dr. Ord, there being no other doctor in the place).[8] The next morning with the consent of the doctor she ate that fatal orange which in a short time brought on vomiting that nothing could stop. Towards night she became better, much better and I laid down towards four in the morning with the full expectation of her recovering. I had hardly got asleep when I was woke up by the doctor. There was no more use for his service. I had to go hunt a priest.

Poor girl, what must have been her feelings while the Priest was going through the last ceremonies of the church, to know that she must die, so young, so beloved, so beautiful, to leave this world to her so gay and happy, with everything around her to make it so: her child, her husband, her parents, and friends without number, for no one ever approached her without loving her, or knew her and her heavenly disposition without adoring her, to separate from all forever to go no one knows where. She was unable to speak, but her eyes when they rested on me told me her feelings too deeply.

Through the whole day she suffered tortures, apparently unconscious of all around her. Every room in the house was

69

filled by her friends who by their tears showed me how great a loss I was about to suffer. Towards evening she for the first time in the day recognized me, called me by name, put out her little hands to embrace me, but with a gentle smile of resignation sunk back on her bed.

All honor was paid her by the inhabitants. I did not attend the funeral but there was hardly a person in the town that did not. Thus by the ignorance of a doctor I have been robbed of a treasure that can never be replaced.

My Negro boy Sam, who has been with me some three years, was so much attached to Manuela that between sadness and drink became crazy. In this state of mind he believed that in the world to come we would all be united once more together. He came into my room one morning, the 8th of April, crying and talking to me about it, and with the intention (as I have since found very good reason to believe) of sending me to join my wife. As I was very busy I ordered him to his room, the door of which opens into mine. He left my room, locked his door, and a few minutes after I heard the report of a pistol. I broke open the door and found him stretched on the floor which with the walls were covered with blood and brains. He had done his work cooly and effectively. Poor boy. He was a faithful servant. He had a black skin but a white heart. Knowing that his affection for my wife was the cause it cast a greater gloom on my spirits.

But I tried to cheer up, thinking that I had another duty to attend to the boy that Manuela had left me. Doña Angustias took charge of it. At first her milk did not agree with it, but with great care and attention it soon recovered. It was beginning to take notice of me and I to center all the love and affection I had for the Mother in him. But this consolation was not to be enjoyed by me. On the night of the 14th it was accidentally killed by its grandmother. She was nursing it in bed, fell asleep. When she woke up he was dead. She had strangled it in her sleep. The doctor persuaded her it died of a convulsion, but to me alone he told the true story.

And now I am once more alone in the world. I know how necessary it is to call on philosophy to bear with all the troubles of the world, but what philosophy can console me? Had these deaths happened in the usual course of world events it would have been bad enough, but to have them caused by ignorance and violence, it is more than I can stand with Christian Fortitude. A few weeks ago we were all so happy, so contented. What a change; would you believe it, even her pet saddle horse has been stolen away. It appears like a judgment from God for some crime that I or her family have committed. But it is impossible for us to judge the actions of God. We must take the world as it comes. There is no remedy. I shall leave this place as soon as I can. I will give up my rancho and mill, for I have no intention now of leaving the army. I shall before I leave erect a tomb to mark the grave of my wife and child.[9] The slab with this inscription I expect soon from San Francisco:

To
Doña Manuela Jimeno
her husband, Don Alfredo Sully, Lieutenant of the
U. S. Army, dedicates this stone as a lasting tribute
and final remembrance of his love and affection.
She died March 28, 1851, at the age of 17
years and five months.
To her son, Don Thomas Manuel Sully, who himself
died, the 15th of April, 1851, at the age of one month.

This I expect soon. As soon as it arrives and is placed I shall bid adieu to Monterey, the happiest and saddest place I have ever lived in, never to return again if I can help it.

With the death of his wife and his infant son, something died in Alfred Sully. He lost the idealism and romanticism of his youth. Rather than let the unhappiness of California prey on his mind, he decided to bury himself in his military career and became a hard-bitten, unemotional soldier.

71

Chapter Four

Alone in Monterey

ALFRED MADE PREPARATIONS TO LEAVE Monterey as soon as possible. He visited Don Manuel and returned the part of the ranch the don had given him. "He pressed me hard to keep it, in fact threw out several inducements for me to do so," Alfred wrote, "but under the circumstances I think the Army the best place for me."

In June he took a trip to Santa Barbara with Doña Angustias to meet his in-laws before he left the country. His trip was spurred by a curiosity to meet the patriarch of the de la Guerra family and "a great desire to see the early places in which lived Manuela, the church where she was confirmed, when in those days she was considered too superior a being to visit the church as the rest of the children did, and a special day and mass was ordered by the Bishop, like some of the old Spanish noblemen we read of."

The trip from Monterey to Santa Barbara took twenty hours. Since it was the first time the doña had been on a steamer, it was a real excursion for her:

We reached Santa Barbara after sunset. As we were not expected it was some little time before the news of our arrival spread over the town. But as the walk up from the beach to the house is near a mile, we were joined by parties of men, women, children, Indians and horses till we accumulated a large procession. I had to go through the ceremony of introduction to any amount of relatives.

At last we reached the house of her Father, Don José de la Guerra y Noriega, as antique a looking pile as you may wish to see.[1] It forms three sides of a square leaving a large courtyard in front facing the street. A heavy portico all around the floors of brick tile, the walls in some places two yards thick. Large folding doors opened into a large hall into which we all entered and were met by the old gentleman, the Doña's two daughters and the rest of the family. The meeting was more sad under the circumstances than pleasing.

The old Don is a queer old specimen of an old Spanish gentleman, very polite, very dignified and very hospitable, but very bigoted and very tyrannical but not unkind. Several of his sons are married and live with their families in the house. As he has an immense amount of property, ranchos, vineyards, cattle, horses, etc., they are occupied in taking charge of things abroad outdoors; but indoors all under his roof obey him as if he were king. To me he was very kind, they say more kind and yielding than is his custom.

Actually, Alfred underestimated Don José.[2] The don was unprepossessing in appearance; he was short, fat, and ugly, with a flat nose and a reserved manner. But he was one of the wealthiest and most influential men in California. He owned 250,000 acres of land, well stocked with cattle; and his vineyards were the finest in the province. Three thousand Indians had built his house in two weeks with timbers that, like the furnishings, had been brought from his native Spain. He was a shrewd trader who kept a quarter of a million dollars in gold in the house for lending and dealing. His charities were legend, and he was the mediator in most local disputes long after he had resigned as alcalde of Santa Barbara.

Don José was not overly fond of Americans, but three of his four daughters married Americans.[3] His sons were to squander the fortune he had amassed as a merchant even before his death. He was an extremely religious man who lived a disciplined life:

The rules and regulations of the house are more strict than a convent. At six prayers and coffee at which I did not attend as they brought me chocolate in bed. Nine, breakfast. Twelve, prayers and dinner, then sleep till four, prayers again and coffee. At nine supper, prayers and all hands to bed. The doors are locked at nine and none suffered to enter after that hour or leave the house. At his table I drank some of the best wine I have ever tasted, made in the houses. A long table at the head of a large room which like the rest was paved with brick and very deficient in point of furniture. At this table were seated the heads of the families and oldest children; and on low benches and on the floor children and their nurses and others of the family. Immense dishes were brought in. . . . One dish one day was an immense bullock head, horns and all, the most delicious thing I have eaten for some time. At another time a lamb entire. In the kitchen were always waiting crowds of poor for their turn.

The don's table boasted a complete silver service for a hundred people. What he could not import, he manufactured in the shops at the rear courtyard of his house.

Alfred found the daughters of the don to be interesting and very pretty; one was sixteen and the other fourteen. He reflected that the youngest was very like Manuela in appearance and manners, although neither one of them could begin to compare with her in poise, intellect, or disposition.

The town I believe has not changed much since first it was built. It is pure California in all its habits. Everybody is related to one another; and in their style of dress they have not changed. I saw some in the old Spanish costume, hair tied up in colored ribbons, velvet jacket and smart clothes. The Mission a mile back on the hill overlooking the town is a noble old building built of sandstone. The head Padre there is an uncle of Manuela's. I was shown the inside of the church which would put to blush many churches in Philadelphia. A splendid old building and to me it was doubly interesting for there in the front is the font at which she was christened; the altar at which she had as a child so often knelt, and at the foot of the altar the tomb of her Grand Mother, who was more than a mother to her. I was there on Holy Thursday, her saint's day. The church was filled & on the same spots knelt her mother and sisters. The solemn music & imposing ceremonies of the church made me very sad. I left the church & walking back of the mission came to the remains of an aqueduct with dams and mills, all in ruins. It is wonderful what those old Spanish priests were able to accomplish with the means at hand. How they civilized the Indians & taught them every branch of useful knowledge & then with the work-men of their own creation erected works that would do credit to any part of the world. There is something in the forms & ceremonies of the Catholic religion that attract the Indian, strikes him with superstitious awe, whereas with our protestant missionary it is first necessary that they should form their mind to make it understand all they wish.

Alfred's sorrowful recollections of his lost wife continued after his return from Santa Barbara. In preparation for his departure from Monterey, he asked his father to paint a picture of Manuela as a gift for the doña, and sent Thomas Sully a daguerreotype.[4] When his father wrote that the picture was on the way and de-scribed it to him, Alfred replied that the "Doña was very sorry to hear that it does not contain my likeness, but I am very glad of it,

Alfred Sully made a pilgrimage to the Mission Santa Barbara shortly after his wife's death. He had "a great desire to see the early places in which

*lived Manuela, the Church where she was confirmed." The trip made him
more sad than satisfied.*

for I don't like the idea of it. She dead appears to me too pure a being to be associated with me here on earth."

T HOUGH HE WANTED TO LEAVE, the army kept Alfred Sully in Monterey for a year and a half after the death of Manuela. Everything in the town reminded him of her; he mentioned her in every letter, and he clung to her memory with a melancholy that bordered on the morbid. Jane, Alfred's sister, painted a picture of Manuela, and he begged her to send it to him. "Don't think the likeness of her will give me pain. The remembrance of her has given me a melancholy pleasure that nothing can drive away, nor do I wish to lose it."

The doña had furnished Manuela's room with the things that had belonged to her, and Alfred spent most of his time there. When her picture arrived from Philadelphia, her friends came "to view it and shed tears over it." He placed a stone over her grave, which had to be put just outside the fence of the Catholic cemetery since she had been married outside of the church.

He relived her funeral when one of her friends died:

We have lately lost another ornament in the town in the death of a young girl who in appearance somewhat resembled Manuela, and her death I believe can be attributed to the same cause —ignorance of the doctor. Her father is an American who has been for many years in the country, married to one of the Vallejos. Her death did not cause as much excitement as that of my wife's, for she was not so universally beloved. The parents being very rich her funeral was solemnized with all the pomp and nonsense of a Catholic country. Her body dressed in white satin, her hair in ringlets and white flowers, was carried through the streets in a pearl-colored satin-lined coffin exposed to the public view with the smoke and incense of lighted tapers and chants by the priests in their gaudy robes. At the church more ceremonies were gone through with. I did not go there to see it. Such sights are disgusting. Her father has placed her outside the burial ground near my wife's body. He says it is a consolation to him to have her near Manuela in death, that the same tree will shadow both their tombs.

Alfred's letters began to take on a more disappointed and negative tone than ever. Describing California's primitive system of law and order, he was cynical:

I suppose you have heard by the papers of the beautiful system of lynch law. It is true that the state of the country—bad laws, bad law givers, and worse executers of the law—rendered this course absolutely necessary for self protection, but I fear they are carrying the matter a little too far, and as is always the case when men get the smell of blood, it is hard to stop them, to bring them into proper state again. We had a case of it here a few days ago. A horse thief in jail, who had threatened to kill. A party broke into the jail at night and strangled the poor devil while he was chained. It was a most horrid sight. I went to see him. They had tied a rope around his neck with five or six turns & fastened the ends around his nose. The rascal deserved death but not in so brutal a manner. It is no wonder that the quiet Californians are disgusted with their new masters. Such actions with the heavy taxes and cheating lawyers will soon drive them out of the country.

He was bored.

Days and nights grind on in the same stale, monotonous mode. I am still in doubts as to when, where and how I shall be disposed of this winter. I hope it will not be my fate to pass it here, though I could not be better provided for than I am at present. Yet Monterey has lost all of its charms for me. May I have the good luck to leave it soon and never put my foot in it

79

Monterey ranch of W. E. P. Hartnell, hide-and-tallow king and father of twenty-five children. Oil by Langdon Sully after a watercolor by Alfred.

again—I never saw a place so changed as this is. You may walk the streets any day and never see a single person. Many houses are without occupants. No parties and apparently no social meetings. I attribute it in a great measure to the death of Manuela, the family and relatives being in mourning who were formerly the head of all amusement.

He was lonely.

I get up at breakfast, light my fire, and take a book and pipe and read and smoke, eat my dinner, read and smoke; eat my supper, read and smoke; go blow out my light and go to bed to begin again the same life tomorrow. Hartnell's family, my cousins, have been caught here in town by the rains as the rivers will not allow them to go back to their ranch. They occasionally visit me and I them; Matilda and Annitte [Anita] being good native girls help somewhat to kill the time. This and the noise of a Dutch family who live under my quarters, who were farmers before Manuela's death, keep me from dying of *tristeza*.

When his quarters in the Cuartel—the government building —were wanted as a hospital, he was forced to look for another place to live. He could not live in the fort, since the government had sent out five hundred recruits in March 1852, and all of the available space was occupied.

The fort is filled, but I don't think it will be so long as they will soon desert. You can't expect soldiers to serve for seven dollars a month when they can get $5 a day as laborers in the country. It's nonsense to think of such a thing and much more to send them out. I am expecting any day to have the pleasure of chasing them all over the country. My new house is a very pretty little cottage near the church, but it is very lonesome.

Doña Angustias had gone to visit her relatives in Santa Barbara, so for the moment he could not go to her house. Because he had no one to visit, he spent his time "conversing with the birds, the flowers and books—quite poetical only it is accompanied by a Meerschaum pipe which is by no means so." When the doña returned, he moved back into her house.

For want of anything better to do I have been amusing myself for the last month as a carpenter for the Doña. Have built her a chicken house, a duck house, a duck pond and various other useful and ornamental affairs. We spend, Doña Angustias and myself, most of the time watching the young ducks diving in the water. But I have another object of interest besides the young ducks. Next door is the Convent of Santa Catalina and by sundry holes in the fence I have a fine view of the nuns in their

81

white robes of the Order of St. Dominico. Among them is a young Mexican girl who resembles very much Manuela, as much in her face as in her manners.

When young she and my wife were playmates. But the poor girl has had a very sad life of it. Her father in a fit of jealousy without the least particle of cause killed her mother. A party of Americans (it being at the time of the war) who were nearby seized him and shot him without judge or jury, but yet very justly. The girl has since been taken under the protection of a California woman who has lately taken the veil and has taken the girl with her into the convent. It would be a very romantic affair to steal her out of the convent and run away with her. Perhaps if I were younger I might be able to do so foolish a thing, but I am old enough now to know that romantic affairs are not always the most prudent.

I am still spending my leisure moments in painting. If you come across anything pretty in a paper or otherwise, cat, dog, horse or cow, send it to me by first opportunity.

I hope we will have a steamer this month, for last month we were entirely without mail, and I suppose some misfortune has happened to her but hope it will not be serious. They have been running their steamers for near two years now without any accident, and it is time for something to happen, as they must be a little careless by this [time], but of course if anything does happen nobody will be to blame; that's the way of doing things nowadays.

Alfred's words proved to be prophetic and close to home. He also had asked his father, Thomas Sully, to paint a religious picture as a gift for Doña Angustias. The artist did a picture entitled "Christ Blessing Little Children" and shipped it by steamer from Philadelphia.

Alfred's correspondence and the research of a twentieth-century journalist explain the painting's hazardous trip to Monterey.

"The picture arrived at last," wrote Alfred. "Started once from San Francisco and the vessel came near being lost and had to put back. At last started on a steamer but steamer being in a hurry loaded her freight on board an old hulk in the harbor which sank." Mayo Hayes O'Donnell told the rest of the story in the *Monterey Peninsula Herald* (September 17, 1955) a century later:

> One day a man walking on the beach came across a large, flat box which had been washed in by the tide. The box bore the name of Doña Jimeno. The finder hastened to the Jimeno home bearing the news. Very soon two stout Indians were sent to bring the box to the abode. Upon opening the outer box and then the tin box, there was found the painting of "Christ Blessing Little Children."

Not a drop of water had reached the picture. Alfred Sully at once recognized his father's work and produced the letter which his father had written him telling of the plans he had for the gift. The picture was passed on to Doña Angustias' daughter, Maria Antonia Lataillade de Orena, and now hangs in a private home in Santa Barbara.

Alfred's life continued to revolve around the Jimeno family. When the doña was ill, he spent four days and nights nursing her, because she felt that only he could turn her in bed. When he heard that the don had offered to sell his ranch for $40,000, he went to Santa Cruz to stop him,

> in which I succeeded. He has now rented it for five years at $10,000 a year, which is cheap, but better for him, for he is a perfect child and don't know how to take care of himself. It is true that it is now none of my business what he does with his property, but yet I dislike to see him cheated by some of my rascally countrymen. His only trouble now is how to get rid in the fastest possible mode of his extra $10,000 a year. He has ordered a new carriage, talks of a trip to New York and building

a home there and a thousand wild and foolish things. Had my wife lived I should have been a rich man in five years. Don Manuel has more land and better than the whole state of Rhode Island, but don't know enough to live in a decent manner. Spends thousands on things he don't want and is economical to a fault in spending for common necessities of life.

On another occasion he told his family:

Since I last wrote to you I have been on a visit to Benicia. I left here on the old Grey, the only member of my last household. Rode that day to the ranch 35 miles, stayed there that night with Don Manuel, next morning rode over to the mill, changed my horse, and rode over to Santa Cruz, where I had business. Next morning I returned to my mill 20 miles. As I rode that distance in 2 hours and a half it was only about 1 o'clock. I concluded to push across the mountains and reach San Jose that night as it was only thirty more miles. I saddled up the old Grey again and started on my journey, but never having been there before I took the wrong trail, & got into a place I thought I never would get out of. The only way to get out was on foot, the horse sliding some of the way down.

After going this way for some two or three miles and meeting a grizzly bear who luckily gave me a wide berth for I had nothing but a packet pistol with me, & going a great ways out of my road, it was 9 o'clock when I reached a small rancho by the side of the road about 8 miles from San Jose. As I had ridden some 50 or 60 miles and wished to spare my horse, I stopped there that night but not to sleep; the fleas would not allow that. I was glad that the crowing of the cocks told me that it was daylight. Soon saddled up and reached San Francisco that afternoon 48 miles. Found the road from San Jose to San Francisco much changed. Yankees and their improvements have made it quite like our country. San Francisco I found in a state of great confusion and dirt. It is sad to see what destruction

the fire has caused, but in many parts it is covered with buildings again, mostly of wood one story high, for the law forbids
building of wood more than 14 feet high; but in many parts
large and handsome buildings of brick are in progress & I doubt
not, if the city can be spared another fire in the meantime, one
year will see it better built than before. I suppose the papers
have given you a full account of the actions of an organized
band of citizens called the Vigilance Committee. They have
done a great deal of good. It no doubt is sad that the state of
society should require such stringent measures, but the laws
while administered by the scoundrels who are now in office are
worse by far than no laws. Everybody walks the street by
night armed.

The world around Alfred continued to change. In late summer
of 1852, Doña Angustias went back to Santa Barbara. "She wants
to live here but her husband, who is a queer sort of chap that don't
know his own mind for two hours, wishes to live in Santa Barbara.
The fact is his two worthy brothers the Friars wish to be near so
they may fleece him and the Doña don't want to go for the same
reason." Instead of going to Santa Barbara, Don Manuel went to
Mexico, taking his two sons with him. He died there in 1853 after
cutting Doña Angustias out of his will.[5] The doña then married
Dr. James Ord, whose qualifications Alfred had criticized so
bitterly at the time of Manuela's death.
Alfred moved into the fort, which was virtually deserted.

I have only one companion, a Mr. Baldwin of Virginia. To
show you how lonely it is, flocks of partridges, or I should say
quails and rabbits, come into the gardens at the fort. As we both
breakfast up there, cooking for ourselves, it is very convenient
for us to take a walk in the garden or around the fort gun in
hand and are sure of killing a good breakfast. One old soldier
that I keep goes down on my horse to town and buys milk and
bread, and Baldwin cooks. I wash the dishes. Dinner I take

wherever I can get it; I suppose you will think this a very poor way of living. It is not the best or the most convenient mode in the world, but as I am expecting to leave I don't wish to enter into any permanent way of messing. At present I am very much occupied putting the government property ready for auction. Grizzly bear tracks are seen on the edge of town, if not in town. Shows you how dull and deserted this place is.

He spent time visiting San Francisco on several occasions.

Plenty of noise there. New York in miniature only more so, but very dirty owing to the late ruins. San Francisco is becoming more settled in its character every day. Many ladies have come out to join their husbands. You find the streets filled now with well dressed ladies and children, which formerly was a rare sight. And in proportion the red shirted pistol gentlemen now decreased. The city is even better than before the fires. They have many beautiful brick homes put and putting up. And as for the rapidity of putting up they beat everything I ever saw. A large brick theatre with iron roof was put up by contract and finished to play in thirty days from laying the foundation. I found some workmen clearing off for a foundation. They told me they were going to build a hotel of brick. I passed there four days after and the brick walls were a few feet above the ground.

For other distractions he hunted wild geese, went on picnics, and watched the changing scene in the harbor.

We have now in port a whaling ship and yesterday I had the satisfaction of seeing them take a whale in the harbor. It was a very exciting scene and I should judge a very dangerous sport. After they harpooned him they were chasing him about the bay for about an hour, a man stationed in the bow of each boat with a lance striking the animal whenever he appeared, till at last he began to spout the red stream from his nose, which I believe is the death signal among whales.

They did not however succeed in killing him till he got on shore among the breakers. The tide has left him high and dry. I had the pleasure of walking on top of him and standing in his mouth like a second Jonas. What a horrid, shapeless piece of black flesh it is. It I understand is quite small being a young one measuring but 50 feet. His mouth is about 15 feet long and filled with small bones like a sieve and an immense tongue. The object of all this as I learnt from the whale men is that sailing along with their mouths open but throat closed with the tongue they scoop up all the fish in the way then by closing the mouth the water is blown out through the sieve, leaving what they scoop up inside. I have a very pressing invitation from the Captain to accompany him in a boat to see the sport, but after what I saw yesterday morning I think I had rather be excused.

During the year and a half he spent in Monterey after Manuela's death, Alfred constantly complained about the lack of law and order, the heavy taxes, cheating lawyers, and, the incompetence of members of both the state and federal legislatures:

The country about here is again infested by a gang of desperate men who have been amusing themselves with robbing and actually killing people, mostly composed of Californians and Mexicans. They were surprised the other day by a party of Americans in pursuit of them, and after a brush they succeeded in securing three of them which they hung on the spot; unfortunately one of them happened to be an innocent man who had the misfortune to be a relation of one of the party and caught in company. Next Friday a man is to be hung for stealing horses. So you see though we have not your operas, theatres, etc., we have other modes of very intellectual enjoyment.

I received yesterday your letters, one from father about money matters.[6] I am astonished that the draft should not have been paid immediately. It was money I was obliged to advance the government about six months ago. At legal interest in this country it should amount to $590, but Uncle Sam never allows interest. He pays his debts when he has money, and when he has none he lets you whistle for it. I think it is quite a commentary on our institutions that a Lieutenant out of his pay is helping to support the expenses of the government. I suppose by this time though you have received the amount as Congress must have settled their disputes and bunkum speeches for making presidents and have attended to their legitimate business like honest men. . . . The Legislature here is still in session, but doing nothing that I can see except to draw their pay of $12 per day and drink whiskey.

His eagerness to get out of Monterey was accentuated by the fact that he was being passed over for promotion.

The list of promotions have arrived. By it I see I am not yet promoted and the reason why is not fully known. You perhaps don't know that the promotions in the army take place in this way: all above the rank of Captain by Corps, the oldest officers first vacancy to the rank of captain, and below by regiment according to vacancies. As the oldest Captain first for Major is in my regiment, his promotion to one of the present vacancies would promote me to his place.

But Congress have been talking about reducing one Major (there are now two) in each regiment and although the law has not yet passed, yet in anticipation of passing next session they have refused to promote any more captains to major. Its a great outrage for them to act so without the law, but might is right, and I suppose I must content myself with my usual bad luck and see some new officers to enter the service two or three years after me promoted before me. I am not strong enough to chop wood and know of no other profession than soldiering so must stick to it.

Alfred had already been promoted to captain more than eight months before this letter was written, but the news had failed to reach him. At last, his great sadness, petty grievances, and ennui were brought to an end when he was ordered back to Benicia in December 1852.

Chapter Five

Return to Benicia

ALFRED WAS AMAZED AT THE CHANGES that had taken place in Benicia since 1849. When Alfred had first come to Benicia, it had been a ghost town, its men gone to the gold fields nearby. But Monterey was being phased out as a military outpost and Commo. Thomas ap Catesby Jones had seen an opportunity to capitalize on this situation for his personal gain. He had moved his fleet to Benicia, on the northern tip of San Francisco Bay, and in concert with Col. Charles F. Smith[1] had had it proclaimed the military and naval headquarters of the Pacific Coast. The federal government had obliged by setting aside almost a hundred acres for a post, to be known as Benicia Barracks; Congress authorized expenditures as extravagant as thirty thousand dollars for single buildings to house the families of only two officers. They had little consideration for the amount of money they spent.

Jones and his friends invested heavily in real estate, and suddenly Benicia became a boomtown. Promoters and speculators went to work. The town that had almost disappeared in 1849 suddenly came to life again. The get-rich-quick schemers made claims that have a familiar ring even today, when a real estate developer gets to work to promote a new piece of land: Benicia was going to compete with San Francisco as a port of entry; its harbor was better than San Francisco's, because it was almost completely landlocked and protected from the sea; Benicia was closer to the mines, and a railroad would be constructed up to Marysville for even closer access to the diggings; a shipbuilding industry had been started; and there was more money to be made from the hotel, restaurants, and stores that would supply and service the workers. The promoters pointed out that inexpensive transportation was already available to San Francisco via the Pacific Mail Steamship Company; with the military and naval base, Benicia would have the full protection of United States forces against encroachment by foreign powers, local felons, or hostile Indians. In 1852, the promoters said, Benicia would not only be the county seat but the capital of the entire state of California. To prove it they built a state house to provide appropriate facilities, and added other amenities, including a church, a Masonic hall, a court house, and a hospital.[2]

The suckers came, and the price of land soared beyond all reason. Fifty-vara lots sold from $500 to $2,000 depending upon the locality and who was doing the trading;[3] a lineal vara varied from 23 to 42 inches, again depending on the trader.

Alfred could see the signs of change even as he approached Benicia. Army stores and ammunition that had been kept out in the open, under rotted canvas, when he had been there before were now kept in secure warehouses that spread out over the land. Adequate barracks had been built for the enlisted men, and there were also quarters for the officers, which looked comfortable from the outside. Nearby were the ways of the shipbuilding company and the slips and piers of the ferries and steamers that plied the bay of San Francisco. Sully had heard of the plans and the boasts, but he viewed them with a jaundiced eye; after all, he had lived in Benicia.

The rich dreams of fabulous customs duties flowing through the hands of city-appointed administrators faded when Benicia failed to be designated as a port of entry. The railroad failed in 1853, and the following year the state capital was moved to Sacramento. Soon the county seat would also change its location.[4]

But Benicia Barracks had been built and it was there to stay. It stood out against the barren background as naked as a railroad station on a long deserted spur. Alfred felt that it was probably the most godforsaken place on the face of the earth. When it was dry, the clay soil hardened and cracked in slits four feet deep. When it rained, the muck was so thick that it was a common sight to see knee boots mired in the roads with just the tops sticking up; their owners had found it impossible to dislodge them. And when it was in between bone-chilling wet and bone-parching dry, the dust blew through the post so that it was impossible to breathe.

Alfred's thoughts went back to Monterey, and for the first time in many months he was glad he was alone and had no one but himself to worry about. The strength of his company had been reduced from 84 to 20 men, and those who had not deserted spent their time on work details, so that military drill was out of the question. Discipline was a sometime thing.

Like the other officers, Alfred at first retreated to the comparative comfort and seclusion of the officers' quarters. About twenty officers were stationed more or less permanently at Benicia Barracks, and transient officers passed through every few weeks. Once again, he began to enjoy the companionship of men with whom he shared common interests on an equal footing. As it had been in the early days at Monterey, life was one continuous party, and whiskey was cheap. Only the girls were missing. "Were I not obliged to go twice a day to the mess room, in which operation I succeed in getting muddy up to my knees and wet all over, I don't think I would ever leave my room."

But he was still a company commander, and he lived with the problems of the enlisted men. Aside from boredom and alcohol, the soldiers' biggest problem was money. They were paid every two months—eleven dollars after the usual slush funds were deducted. Out of that they had to buy fresh vegetables or risk contracting scurvy—army rations did not include fresh foods. Alfred sympathized: "The commonest sort of low drunken blackguard can earn that amount in two days."

The officers fared no better. Their mess bill was barely covered by their pay. Alfred resorted to speculating in things he thought were safe—horses, land, and gold—the things which he thought he could turn over quickly if by some good fortune he was ordered out. More fortunate officers had nest eggs of two or three thousand dollars, which they lent out at interest rates of 5 percent per month. Those who had no savings—particularly the three officers on the post who were married—were constantly borrowing, and getting deeper and more hopelessly in debt. They lived from day to day in hopes that the army could not enlist new recruits for the Pacific Coast because of the pay scale; that all of the enlisted men would soon desert, and that the government would then be forced to call the troopless officers back east.

Their dilemma was not helped when gold became harder to find, and coin became more scarce. Prices skyrocketed.

I returned the other day from a visit to a friend of mine, a former captain in the army who has changed his sword for a plow. I found him hard at work on his ranch, but quite contented. I asked him if he did not regret his having resigned, but he was far from that. "Why," says he, "the sale of eggs from my chickens pay me better than the government did in this country after having served them faithfully seventeen years." I believe him. It would only take two dozen eggs a day to do that now.

Alfred heard that his former ranch in Monterey had sold for $36,000 in cash, and it gave him cause to ponder. With little military duty and a great deal of time on his hands, he began to think more about money and the inequity of his situation, and he realized that if he stayed in the army, he would need political pull in Washington in order to improve his situation. He saw a great deal of tangible evidence of this.

The navy was doing all right by its people, who had just received an increase in pay retroactive to 1846, but Congress ignored a bill to increase army pay. The navy seemed to scoff at gross improprieties on the part of its officers. Commodore Jones, who had started the Benicia boom, was found to have taken government funds and bought gold at eight dollars, reconverted it to government coin at twelve, and then pocketed the difference. His excuse was that the merchants needed the coin. Although he was arrested and "convicted in 1851 for speculating in gold dust and sentenced to suspension from the Navy for five years with loss of pay for half of that time," he was released and returned to Benicia the following year in command of all naval forces on the Pacific Coast.

As collector of customs in Monterey, Alfred had had $200,000 in civil funds on deposit in his accounts. He was offered the same deal that Jones had made, and the temptation was great. "Would that I had known at the time that the government would have sanctioned such acts, I might have been better off. Politics, politics, nothing but politics in every transaction of our government."

But he felt that this was dishonest. He steadfastly refused to use government funds for his own gain in any way; he never speculated unless he used his own cash and could afford the loss; he never borrowed money, and apparently never gambled. He resigned himself to the fact that he would never be wealthy, although he always had some legitimate get-rich-quick scheme in mind; he concluded that "what can't be cured must be endured." At the same time, he decided that he must be more selective in his choice of friends if he wanted to attain any rank in the army.

Alfred's feelings were not unique. An air of hopelessness and uncertainty pervaded the officers' quarters, and most of them turned to drink. Whiskey was cheap and it made the time pass.

Lt. George Crook, who was to become a major general in the Civil War, was fresh out of the military academy at West Point and was quartered with the officers of two companies of Alfred's regiment at Benicia. Crook wrote in his diary:

94

The officers, as near as I can recollect, were Major Day,[5] Captain Frazier, Lieutenants Steele[6] and Fighting Tom Wright,[7] 2nd Infantry; Scott and Underwood, 4th Infantry. With the exception of Captain Frazier and Steele there was not a day passed but what these officers were drunk at least once, and mostly until the wee hours of the morning. I have never seen such gambling or carousing before or since. My first duty after reporting was as a file closer to the funeral escort of Major Miller[8] 2nd Infantry, who had just died from the effects of strong drink. Major Day, whose head was as white as the driven snow, commanded the escort, and when all of us officers had assembled in the room where the corpse was lying, he said, "Well fellows, Old Miller is dead and can't drink, so let us all take a drink." I never was so horrified in my life.

Alfred shared the other officers' taste for drink, but he felt that he could better occupy his time.

His thoughts constantly drifted back to Monterey, and he kept hoping that he could recapture some of the romance and happiness he had found there. In June of 1853, he went back for a visit. His old friends and in-laws begged him to resign from the army and stay there permanently. For sentimental reasons he almost did. In the past, he had expressed the wish to settle in California and the inducements offered were many. But now he realized that Monterey would never be the same—nor would he. In place of the peaceful harbor surrounded by tree-topped hills and the scent of pine and salt air, Alfred found a fishing port with all the noise, odor, and commotion of a large commercial operation. "The place was filled with Chinamen, catching fish and abalone. These they ship to San Francisco to be consumed by their countrymen. I suppose at and near Monterey there must be at least three hundred of them. It looks like a second Canton and smells like a fish market."

Any doubt left in his mind as to whether he should still dream of returning to Monterey with occasional trips to San Francisco or

On Alfred's occasional trips from Benicia to San Francisco, he frequently whiled away the hours sketching ships and sailors.

Benicia was dispelled not only by his visit to Monterey but also by his trip back to San Francisco in June, 1853. The steamer he took was the first available, a small boat overloaded with

> about eighty of these dirty, foul smelling Chinese. The laborers were paid a dollar a day while the four head men reaped a profit of twenty dollars a day from fish on each man under them. When the boat began to pitch and roll in the ground swells off the California coast the passengers began to sicken and panic. The ship was overladen with potatoes, a cargo that the captain did not want to lose. Under pressure the pumps broke and every man on board ship was forced to take a turn at bailing with buckets to keep the ship from sinking. While the men bailed for their lives the captain loaded up the fires and put on as much steam as possible, so we had the anticipation of blowing up if we did not go down.

The trip that normally took eight hours took twenty-four. Alfred never went back to Monterey, nor did he ever mention Manuela or the don again except in a very brief autobiography he wrote about twenty years later.

He found that he could go down to San Francisco by steamer in three hours for a dollar. He went often but did not stay long because he could not afford it. "There's a young friend of mine here in the barracks who spent $250 in less than a week and did not know how he did it."

The city was vital. It drained away his loneliness and made him feel alive. He saw in it the east, "a second New York but with a great deal more excitement and bustle." He watched it being built "Venice-like" into the sea and likened it to the Atlantic docks in Brooklyn. Again, everything was "let her rip," and he wondered where it would end. Here is how he described the city in 1852:

> Yet San Francisco is improving very much. There was a time

when $10 would not have bought you a decent meal. But it is surprising to see with what rapidity people have sprung up from the lowest walks of society; every time I walk the streets I meet with some wonder of this kind. The other day a young man of about 26 years old stopped me and asked if I did not recollect him. He proved to be the son of a miserable little village tailor in Sacketts Harbor. He took me to his store, a fine two story brick grocery establishment with his name in fine big gold letters over the door, Whitemore and Gladden. He is doing a fine business that many of our first merchants would envy, and will without doubt in a few years be immensely wealthy. He is only one of the many wonders of the kind you meet with every day.

But as much as he enjoyed the "anything goes" attitude of a two-fisted city coming alive, as much as he wanted to be part of it—just as he had wanted to be part of the Monterey that used to be—Alfred felt alone there. Only his sense of humor kept him sane. When his family worried because Sacramento was four-fifths under water, and the hotel had to be entered by boat from the second story while a steamer went up and down the main street,[9] he wrote back:

What do you think of its raining meat? . . . On a clear bright day, pieces of meat the size of your finger, some of them, fell to the earth. Their fall was witnessed by about twenty persons. About half a bushel or more fell. This to a superstitious person might be considered a great phenomena, but it is easily accounted for by being disgorged by some vultures very high in the air out of sight, as is frequently the case when pursued by eagles.

At this point in his life, Alfred did not care what happened, just as long as something did happen. He was still in love with Monterey and excited by San Francisco, but he knew he would never fit into either place.

Benicia was only a stopping-off point. Latrine rumors flew thick and fast: his company was going to be sent north to fight the Indians in Oregon; the government could not afford to keep troops in California, so they would all be sent home again; he might be called back to Washington to account for the quartermaster records that had piled up for five years; or they might all go back to Mexico to fight Santa Anna again. Alfred did not care what happened so long as he got away from Benicia.

A GROUP OF ILL-ADVISED, hotheaded men in Oregon determined Alfred's next move. In spite of the influx of miners and settlers through Oregon, there were no regular army forces stationed there. The protection of emigrant trains and settlers against the Indians, on whose land they encroached, was left to volunteer troops and militia. One such company, organized in Yreka, California,[10] under Capt. Ben Wright, lured about fifty leaders of the Modocs, neighbors of the Rogue River Indians, into camp for a feast which was to precede a peace council. Once the Indians were unarmed, Wright's men calmly murdered forty of them.[11] Other Modocs and neighboring tribes retaliated, and raids and depredations became frequent.

Alfred sympathized with the natives:

The Indians are again becoming troublesome. A fine officer, Lieutenant Russell[12] lost his life the other day, killed by Indians of the Sierra Nevada. You can't blame the Indians. They are frequently killed out of sport by these rascally whites and of course they retaliate. I do think our race of Western Missouri men, commonly called Pike's County Men, are the most unmitigated, mean, rascally race I ever met with. They have all the meanness of the low Yankee, combined with the

99

ignorance and laziness of the negro and the brutality of the Indian.

In June 1853, a few months after the death of Lieutenant Russell, a group of white settlers near Jacksonville, just south of the Rogue River, heard a rumor that the Indians had captured two white women. They hanged three Indians, shot seven more, and went out to celebrate their heroism by getting drunk.

The Indian raids on the nearby white settlements became more frequent, until finally the whites stopped all business, fortified their houses, howled for troops and ammunition, and went out to hunt Indians. Two hundred men were formed into a force under the leadership of Capt. Bradford R. Alden, the commander of Fort Jones in Scott's Valley, at the northern border of California.[13] By the time Alden reached what was to be the scene of the battle, rumors had circulated among his volunteers that the Indians were raiding white settlements, and the militiamen dispersed to protect their homes. He came to the Rogue River battle with only ten men.[14]

At about the same time, another group of about a dozen volunteers had been formed by Governor Joseph Lane. Lane was a glory-seeking politician, who between terms as governor of Oregon, had served as a congressman in Washington. Having had some experience in minor brushes with the Indians, he fancied himself as an Indian fighter and had himself named a brigadier general of the Oregon Volunteers, over the protest of some of his colleagues. In spite of the fact that he had had no military training, he assumed command over Alden, a West Point graduate.

Alfred's was one of three units ordered to proceed from Benicia to the Rogue River to reinforce the militia. Normally the strength of this force should have been 254 men. But desertions, expired enlistment terms, and a lack of replacements had reduced it to about 60.

The troops went up the Sacramento River by steamboat for one hundred miles to Colusa.

From there we marched over a horrid dusty road to Shasta 120 miles, to the mountains and gold mines over two or three chains of mountains in a northerly direction with a pleasant variety of snow, rain and fatiguing mountains to climb. Passing through the town of Yreka and marching some 200 miles more from Shasta, we reached at last the valley of the Rogue River in Oregon and the scene of action. We passed through some of the most splendid scenery among which must be mentioned Mount Shasta the highest peak in our country. . . . One half is always covered with snow. I would have enjoyed the trip had I not suffered much from blistered feet, and having caught like the rest the chills and fevers. None who pass through the valley of the Sacramento ever escape it. Luckily I only suffered two or three days when I reached Fort Jones in Scotts Valley and there the Doctor cured me in a few days by drinking down some quinine.

Army records show that Alfred's company had a few minor skirmishes with the Indians on the Rogue River. But through all his years of Indian campaigns and Civil War Battles, Alfred was loath to mention to his family very much about his personal safety in combat, other than to assure them that he was unharmed. His letters from Oregon gave no hint of the fact that sickness and the elements were not the only things that concerned him and his skimpy force. There was the dread of fighting the Rogue River Indians. These Indians were reputed to be excellent marksmen who could put an arrow through a man at sixty yards and could keep an arrow in the air from this distance at all times while the soldiers were readying their muzzle-loading guns for a second shot. Apprehension was further increased by the knowledge that the Indian arrows had small barbed points fastened to the heads with moistened sinews; when this sinew came in contact with warm blood it melted, and the barbs remained in the body when the arrow was withdrawn.[15]

These were typical examples of the kind of scuttlebutt that

passes through the ranks whenever a soldier faces battle. As usual, the anticipation was worse than the reality. By the time Sully's unit arrived the fighting was about over.

From General Lane and others he pieced together the story of the battle he had missed:

Captain Alden and his men were the only troops to get forward and he was shot for his trouble. General Lane with a few volunteers comes to the rescue, while the rest of the gallant volunteers are all stationed behind trees where there is no danger of their being hit or hitting anybody. They then conclude much against the wishes of General Lane (who wishes to go forward) to make a treaty.

As soon as the treaty is made and while the rest of the Indians are in camp, assisting the whites who are wounded, up marches a reinforcement of citizens and the warlike spirit of the whites is roused to such a pitch that it is with the greatest difficulty Lane prevents his men from falling upon the Indians and murdering them. "Damn the Indian. Take advantage of him while you can," is the cry of these brave Americans.

There was quite a difference between what Alfred learned on the scene from the participants and what Lane reported to the government in Washington.

If you read his official report in the papers you would think there never were such brave troops in the world as these same cowards. But you see, he is a member of Congress, is obliged to write this way for political reasons. I could write all night accounts of the cruelty and barbarity of these human beings that would hardly be believed at home and yet government will pay these men $8 a day for their services (some 200 of them) and only give a soldier seven dollars a month. Yet this is all done for political reasons.

Alfred was glad to see three companies of dragoons arrive in the valley, even though their strength was only seventy men, for it meant that his company was relieved and ordered to return to Benicia, "for which I thank my good fortune. The others have to pass the winter there with the Indians. I left them building log huts, for the snow falls to a depth of six feet, and was glad to turn my way south. The three hundred miles over the mountains were marched in two weeks."

Alfred Sully did not get his baptism of fire in the Rogue River expedition, but he learned that the soldier's worst enemy is fear. He began to appreciate the hardships a foot soldier must endure in a forced march under adverse conditions, and for future reference he knew how hard he could drive his men. He also had the time to do the illustrations for a journal kept by one of the members of his detachment.[16]

He described his Oregon trip in a letter to his sister Blanche dated November 1, 1853. In the same letter he told her that he wanted to take a leave and go home but that it would cost nearly $1,000 and he could not afford it. Two weeks later he received orders to return to New York City.

Chapter Six

Forts on the Frontier

ALFRED LEFT CALIFORNIA in 1853 to begin a new chapter of his life, one that would form him into the tough, duty-bound soldier he had inwardly determined to become since his losses in Monterey. He was so relieved to get away from California that he did not care where he went or how he got there. He just wanted to go, and the army sent him the worst possible way.

He sailed from San Francisco on a ship that was subsequently wrecked on a rocky island off the coast of California, where he spent ten uncertain days before he was picked up and sent on his way again. At this point he learned that he would not go around Cape Horn, but across the Isthmus of Panama.

The very word *Isthmus* brought terror into the hearts of the bravest of men and women. It was often compared to the Natchez Trace, the old New Orleans road where murder and throat-cutting were common, but the Isthmus had an even worse reputation. It had malaria, cholera, and yellow fever, and dysentery was reputed to have killed off almost half of the people who crossed it.

But by taking the Isthmus route, the gold-hungry could reach

California in half the time. Alfred, too, was willing to take his chances if the Isthmus would get him home sooner.

The city of Panamá was on the southern side of the Isthmus. Ship after ship came in and was immediately loaded with gold-seekers who refused to get off even though they had no tickets. Ship space was so scarce that baggage, including his, was dumped overboard to make room for passengers. Nevertheless, some four thousand men were stranded in the place, some for months.[1] Soon there were saloons, gambling dens, and whorehouses. Alfred was glad to leave Panamá. But the trip north was no great joy (the Panama Canal was more than half a century away). An improvised railroad ran about fifty miles northwest, to the mouth of the Las Cruces River, and on its little cars Alfred shook out his insides, dreaming of a good night's sleep and a clean place in which to bed down, as well as a meal that might be at least digestible.

To get any meal was a battle. There were long rows of tables, and a meal cost a dollar. Alfred saw that his only chance of getting fed was to be at the end of the table, for by the time the platters reached the middle there was nothing left. So he was ungentle-manly enough to bump the man off the end and grab the platter first. His stomach stuffed, though with not the freshest of food, he contemplated a good night's sleep. But this was not to be had at Las Cruces. The only available space was in a barracks-type building with triple-deck bunks. Most of his fellow lodgers were miners returning from California without their bonanzas but with an ample supply of brandy. Whenever the spirit moved them, they would rise from their bunks, sing lusty and bawdy songs, and fall back into their sacks too drunk to stagger.

To add to the confusion, at one end of the barracks building there was a thin wall behind which slept the prostitutes, hangers-on who followed the gangs building the railroads. Loud conversation between the men and the women ran on all night, and the sharing of beds was not just a sometime thing.

Alfred got no sleep and was disgusted with the whole business. He was not exactly a prude, but he did like to take his amorous adventures in something akin to privacy, and the idea of entertaining a lewd woman with a male audience to cheer him on was more than abhorrent to him. He punched his hand in his pillow and tried to cover his ears and get some sleep, but the loud grunts and groans and giggles penetrated the pillow.

He was relieved when morning came, and he started the trek from Las Cruces along the old Spanish Trail to Portobello. But his mule was stubborn, and no amount of whipping would make him head for the barn. By the end of half a day Alfred was glad to rid himself of his beast of burden and board the comparative comfort of a ship headed for home.

He was looking forward to visiting his family in Philadelphia. The ties in the Sully family had always been very close. Morally, Thomas Sully was an exceptionally strong man. His children regarded him with affection and esteem, and their lives were very much controlled by what they thought he might feel. This devotion was typified by a tender note his daughter Jane sealed and tucked into his drawer when she fell in love:

When you were in Baltimore about sixteen or eighteen months ago I gave you a promise in one of my letters to make you, my dear father, my confidant whenever I should form an attachment for anyone. I need not name whom I mean. I am sure you can easily guess. We have determined to be directed by you in all things and I could not feel justified until I told you. If you dislike the choice I have made tell me so and I will do my best to forget I ever knew him. I have always made up my mind to obey you in everything I do. Henry intended speaking to you but I thought that perhaps that you would like better to hear it from your own child. If this offends you dear father, forgive me. If you tell my mother which perhaps you may, request her to keep my secret from everyone.

Your J —.

I would rather you would write me an answer and leave it in my drawer.

Blanche Sully, Alfred's sister, painted by
Thomas Sully when she was twenty-five.

Thomas approved, and Jane was married to William Henry Darley in 1833.

Alfred thought warmly of his sisters as he sailed for home, especially Blanche. To her he wrote his letters home, and to her he looked for the strength that would be needed by the rest of the family if Thomas Sully should predecease her.

Thomas Sully depended on her, too. Although he never made a great deal of money, from what little he had, he denied his children nothing that he could afford to give them. He loved his wife and all of his children, but when it came time for him to go to England to paint his celebrated portrait of Queen Victoria, it was Blanche he chose to go with him and take care of him; and it was Blanche who looked after his wants until the day he died.

Alfred's only brother, Thomas, had been very much the roué

and man-about-town, talented as an artist and beloved by the ladies, but by his father's own admission totally lacking in responsibility and the other qualities he so admired in Alfred and Blanche. Thomas Sully, Jr., died tragically in 1847, at the age of thirty-six.

Alfred enjoyed his visit home. He fended off questions about Manuela, and in time he had to retreat to his father's studio to escape the many feminine attentions poured upon him. Thomas was interested in Alfred's marriage, but his sense of delicacy prevented his probing. They talked about politics, and they talked about money. Thomas advised his son to set aside enough money for retirement, not realizing that the military would take care of that. By this time Alfred's only ambition was to make a good career for himself in the army; oddly enough, he was no longer interested in making money.

He was concerned about what he might find on the frontier. Desertions from the army had been common and had resulted in a reduction in strength that would be hard to fill. It was only the commissioned and noncommissioned officers who had been ordered to the East Coast to "recruit their companies"[2] and to get ready for duty on the western frontier after the new men had been trained. Alfred explained to his father that he had only a few weeks to do this. Then he had to be on his way.

Satisfying as it was to be home, he was nonetheless anxious to leave. Philadelphia palled, just as Monterey and Benicia had; Alfred had a restless core that drove him constantly to seek something different. He did not like to be pampered, and he looked forward to life in the field. But he went along with his family, letting them make the most of the time he had available before he had to leave.

Wondering wistfully how many of his sisters he would ever see again, Alfred assembled what men he had recruited and started for the western frontier. He did not know it at the time, but service in Benicia had been a pink tea party compared to what he would face in the next six or seven years.

The frontier was vaguely described as west of the Mississippi and north of St. Louis. In less than a decade the United States had almost tripled its miles of territory—territory avidly taken by miners and farmers who had to trespass on Indian lands if they wanted to cross through or wrest the lands from the Indians by force if they decided to stay. In either case, units like Alfred's had to convoy the emigrant trains or to protect the settlements with forts and provide a meager line of supply for themselves and for those just passing through.

When Alfred left for the frontier in July 1854, he resented the emigrants. He regarded them as freeloaders, looking for profits and demanding government protection while they looked. As Alfred watched, forts grew up "like Topsy." Whenever a political voice was powerful enough to be heard in Washington, demanding protection for people or property in any location along the vast frontier, whether that particular location fitted basic military needs or not, there the army was told to build a fort. Alfred began to realize that soldiers were just pawns in the political scheme of things—and as pawns they were expendable.

A company or two would be marched out into the wasteland, given picks, shovels, axes, and saws, and told to build a fort. Sometimes the nearest wood was a day's or even two days' march away. Forage for the animals and food for the men was a constant problem. But if a fort must be built, it always was.

While Alfred was first a soldier and then an artist, he was also an engineer and a builder. The forts he helped to build or to improve for the most part stood defenseless on the open prairie or clung hopefully to the questionable shelter of a hillside that might be indefensible. They were made of mud and clay, rude cottonwood logs and tarpaper, and sometimes of thin sheets of prefabricated material brought in by riverboats.

Few of these so-called forts had stockades or blockhouses. Sully accepted the fact that they were built to move ahead of the waves of emigrants, subsist on the crest, and be swept aside in the surf when the tide had passed. At first his men spent more time

109

as common laborers than they did as fighting soldiers. They dug post holes, cut logs, made rough hewn planks, baked bricks, cleared brush, built latrines, hauled supplies, fed and cared for horses and mules, and did the thousand and one things a man must do to "build a fort." His was not an isolated experience. More than seventy small outposts, dignified by the name of "fort" but long since forgotten, were the army's first line of defense on the western frontier. Sully recognized that they were more like supply dumps, open for the taking, than citadels. Even the primary army concerns for sanitation, eating, and sleeping facilities were often secondary in the desperate attempts to set up a base of supply, establish a show of strength, and provide a seeming haven for the migrant citizen.

His soldiers knew that both their current duty and the forts they built and occupied were temporary. They were held together during the winter months by a common bond of dependency upon each other, if by nothing else. In California the men had found it easy to desert. They could subsist on the land, hope for finds in the gold fields, make a touch when they were down on their luck, or—all else failing—return to their units.

But it was a different story in the Dakotas, Minnesota, and Nebraska. There were no friends to take them in, no handouts for deserters. If they left their unit and managed to survive the elements, they would be killed by those Indians who did not lean on the forts for annuities. Summer or winter, there was no place to go and no way to get there. No man—no small group of men— could subsist without food or shelter in a wilderness where temperatures dropped to thirty below zero or rose to heights that left parched animals to die by the side of the trail. His men stayed together out of sheer necessity—and because he ruled them by fear tempered at times with a feeling of compassion. Stern discipline was a matter of course; it was mandatory for keeping the men alive.

The frontier service suited his quest for challenge, novelty, and above all the sobering plunge into basic soldiery that would keep his mind from Manuela. While he was away from his post on patrol, about fifteen of the men he left behind—20 percent of his depleted command—took a chance and deserted. He brought them back. When he returned and assumed command again, virtually everyone drew extra duty and the desertions ceased.[3]

He allowed the men to live like Indians. They dressed in hides and beaver caps and mittens. They slept in buffalo robes, which their Indian friends would provide for three dollars apiece. If they were lucky enough to have bread, they kept it close to their bodies even while they slept, to prevent it from freezing so solid that even an axe would not cut it thin enough to be edible.

There were usually Indian encampments near the forts in the area then known as the Northwest Territory, and Alfred was surprised to note that the Indians came and went as they pleased —inside the forts or out of them. They begged what food they could from the officers or soldiers who had rations from the government stores. The soldiers in turn frequented the Indian tents and slept with the Indian women. The tepees had fires in the center and wind-tight walls closed at the base with banks of brush or snow. The body warmth of many occupants made these teepees far more comfortable than the crude barracks, which had makeshift walls and floors of flimsy wood raised from the ground, or earthen floors that froze hard in spite of the soldiers' pitiful attempts to heat their sleeping quarters.[4]

While their primary concern was simply to survive, the soldiers under Alfred's command had to patrol an almost boundless area. The need to be in three or four places at once made it necessary for him and his men to march more than a hundred miles a month in subzero weather; mules, horses, and men were reported frozen to death on many a patrol. One regiment marched almost twenty-five hundred miles from Fort Leavenworth to the Columbia River in Oregon without sighting a single house.[5]

Alfred calculated that, even with increases in authorized strength, fewer than 13,000 men had to provide security for immigrants, settlers, and prospectors over an untamed country of more than 3,000,000 square miles. His resentment against the citizens with their cumbersome wagons that he had to protect grew stronger week by week. But as a soldier he continued to perform his duties—exploring the land ahead of him and mapping it, blazing trails, building roads and forts, and trying to keep hostilities with the Indians at a minimum. As a man with a command he was not alone. Others like him were aware of the fact that by 1860 there were only 198 companies in the service. The average strength of a company was about sixty men. There were 183 companies spread out over 79 frontier posts; the other 15 were comfortably stationed along the Atlantic coast, in 23 arsenals, and along the Canadian border.[6] Alfred and his counterparts began to resent more and more their function of playing wetnurse to a bunch of land-grabbers and adventurers whose interest was only in profit to themselves. Alfred and his fellow officers began to question the motives and ability of civilians back in Washington to run the army on an unbiased basis.

But having recognized the situation, they still had to accept it. They were soldiers who had been given a tough job to do and only the tough would survive. Even at this point many believed that there would be a war between North and South, and they were giving much thought as to which side they should be on. This feeling gave new meaning to discipline and physical conditioning. By the time the Civil War actually broke out, Alfred's men would be efficient, stoical soldiers who had learned to obey orders without question and who would become the backbones of the units to which they were assigned.

Not all of the forts were the lean-tos or vulnerable outposts described above. Some, like Fort Laramie in Wyoming, Fort Snelling in Minnesota, and Fort Leavenworth in Kansas—all on the main routes to Oregon and Wyoming—were well built, well fortified, and well supplied. They were stopping-off places where emigrants, pioneers, or adventurers could rest, regroup, and get fresh supplies. Sully's duties took him to the best as

In August 1855, Gen. William S. Harney set out from Fort Kearny to attack the Sioux, brutally murdering men, women, and children.

well as the worst of these outposts.

His first station, in 1854, was at Fort Ridgely, Minnesota. High on a bluff overlooking the Minnesota River, Ridgely was to be a model for such western forts as Fort Phil Kearny, Fort Abraham Lincoln, and others. Included in its design was a parade ground ninety yards square, with a two-story barracks building made of stone on one side; a stone warehouse and commissary were at right angles to it; and at right angles to that were officers' quarters, a bakery, post headquarters, and the facilities for the post surgeon.

It was built in a U shape with the open end of the U commanding a sweeping view of the river 150 feet below. When he first saw the site Alfred felt that it was impregnable. Between the base of the bluff and the river was a stretch of three quarters of a mile that could be peppered by fire from the fort. To the north, or open side of the U, it commanded an unobstructed view of the prairie for as far as firepower could reach.[7]

The land around was fertile. It was to produce an onion that measured more than five inches in diameter, turnips the size of small pumpkins, and a rutabaga that weighed more than nineteen pounds. The alfalfa was so strong that its roots could penetrate ten feet of clay, so clover for the cattle was no problem. Cranberries, grapes, and wild fruits grew in abundance.

Ridgely had stables, granaries, root cellars, and haystacks. It was a monument to the engineering skill, ingenuity and dedication of the men who built it with nothing but crude tools, blood, sweat, and blisters.[8] Even though some of its twelve or more buildings were built of wood, its lifespan would be longer than that of most forts because of its strategic location.

Ridgely was founded in 1853. When Alfred and his company arrived a year later the fort was still under construction and they were assigned to work on the building of it.

Even as he helped to build it, Alfred knew that in time Ridgely would be bypassed by the changing tide. Again he did not mope over this, but it added to the stoicism that would mark his future military life. His only consolation was to come from the fact that he would be able to use it as a base for his military operations and campaigns against the Indians of the Northwest.

While the comfortable new quarters were being built, Alfred and his men were in temporary, inadequate shelters. Some of their time was spent fighting Indians and Alfred seemed to enjoy these brief respites from the construction work. On May 28, 1855, he wrote:

Six Companies of our Regiment take post at Fort Pierre 250 miles west of here on the Missouri. We are congratulating ourselves, having past a hard Winter here & nothing to eat, upon the prospect of nothing to do this Summer but to cultivate our gardens and prepare for Winter; but if the report of an Indian runner is true, we are like to have mostly work. He says all the hostile Indians are crossing the Missouri and are on their way to Lake Traverse, 100 miles north of this place. The Indians around us are the same nation (the Sioux) as those that kicked up the last shindig. They are generally however disposed to be quiet, but among all these bands there are some rascals who, feeling themselves somewhat incensed at the unjust manner in which they have been treated by government agents, are somewhat disposed to take a hand in whatever game turns up.

A short time ago some of them cut the throat of a white man, robbed his farm and burnt his house. This happened about 150 miles from here. If we had horses we might have succeeded in capturing some of the red devils. As it was, hearing that some of them and a party of (other) Indians were down the river at a halfbreed's house I was started off in the evening after them. I sent a party on the other side of the river under a Lieutenant and with both parties moved down the river banks. We had a delightful time of it all night: rain, thunder and lightening, nothing to drink or smoke. I wished myself at the corner of 10th and Chestnut or Billy Shinn's. And what was worse, we found the murderers had cut stick. We however kept the Chief of the band to which they belonged (Mr. Sleepy Eyes) a prisoner. The other day he got tired of being locked up so made a break for tall timber. The sentinel in charge of him invited him to stop and not liking the discourteous manner in which he treated his invitation taught him politeness by planting a ball and three buckshot in his stern sheets. Even after he was shot he was disposed to make a fight of it, and it was not until he had had two trials of the hardness of the musket in communion with the head that he suffered himself to be taken back to his quarters.

It was not long before he received orders to march his unit (Company F, Second Infantry Regiment) from Fort Ridgely to Fort Pierre in what was then Nebraska Territory. Here he was to get his first bitter taste of outpost life on the open plains.

In the summer the wind swept hot and strong across the territory Alfred had to cross, whipping up fine sand and dust that scorched the eyeballs and pitted the skin. He had to make sure that stragglers did not fall so far behind that they might be picked

115

The wind blew a death-dealing cold at Fort Pierre. It had no wood
for heating, no forage for animals, no ground for cultivating.

off by the Indians. A marching infantry was no match for the
Sioux on their fast ponies, and Sully worried that an attack could
come on a four-hundred-mile trek. But none came and his biggest
problem was keeping up the morale of his men and fighting the
elements. He knew that if the men ever felt that they were close
enough to a settlement where they could get cheap whiskey and
loose women, some of them would desert. His primary concern
was to reach his destination with a full complement of healthy
men. So he drove his unit unmercifully, thinking that this was
the only way to maintain morale and keep them going. Pack
animals dropped by the side of the road and had to be shot.

Sully promised his men a haven when they reached Fort
Pierre—a haven against the summer's sun and heat and winds
and sand, and a promise of protection when winter came and they
knew the temperature would drop to thirty below. So they
trudged the four hundred miles from Fort Ridgely to Fort Pierre
with belief in their leader and with hope for better things to come.

When they finally did reach Fort Pierre, Alfred got a shock that would have made a lesser man give up. The fort was an uninhabitable shambles. If there had been anywhere to run he probably would have lost half his command. But there was no place to go.

On paper Fort Pierre was considered to be an ideal spot from which to launch the proposed campaigns in the Dakotas, Nebraska, and Minnesota. Alfred was advised by army intelligence that boats with supplies, troops, and ammunition could travel up the Missouri River from St. Louis to Pierre for about three months out of the year; the rest of the year low water and ice made the Missouri impassable. He realized that in spite of the limited time during which it was accessible by river, the fort had other strategic advantages: Fort Laramie was only 325 land miles to the west; Pierre would be a good base from which to extend forts all along the Missouri to the north and west; it was close to the Black Hills and had access through the Cheyenne River. Finally, the fort was already built.

Viewed from the desk of a politician in Washington, Fort Pierre was undoubtedly an ideal base for all operations against the hostile Indians in the Northwest.

There was only one problem. No man empowered to make a decision as to its usefulness had ever seen it when the government acquired it. Fort Pierre had been built by the American Fur Company in 1832 as a trading post. The company palmed it off on the government as an army post in April 1855 for $45,000.

When Maj. William R. Montgomery[9] arrived to take command of the post in August, he was overwhelmed by the magnitude of the problem that faced him. Pierre consisted of a group of rat-infested, broken down, old wooden buildings unfit for human habitation. There were holes in the walls where the dust blew through in sufficient quantity to choke a man to death. The floors were too thin or rotted to support a man's weight. The wooden walls had been eaten away by insects. There was no mess hall or adequate latrine facilities, hence the horrible odor. All the wood and grass had been stripped away for eight miles and it was difficult to find forage for the animals. With winter fast coming on and the probability of a drop in temperature to thirty degrees below zero, Montgomery violated one of the basic precepts of army command: when in a seemingly impossible situation, the only mistake you can make is not to do anything. Montgomery did not do anything. He made no attempt to provide adequate protection against the elements but let the men fend for themselves while he waited for the arrival of Gen. William S. Harney, who was in command of all operations against hostile Indians in the area.[10] Alfred and his men made woefully unsuccessful attempts to patch up the holes with the minimal materials available. They could not build the necessary latrines or mess hall without orders and materials, and neither of these was forthcoming.

Harney arrived at Fort Pierre on October 19. He was a rough campaigner who had seen service in the Seminole Indian War and the war with Mexico, and he was in a bad mood because he had just needlessly massacred Indians at Ash Hollow.[11] For this inglorious victory he was being roundly criticized, not only by Congress and civilians, but even by army men themselves. He had only been following his basic philosophy as far as the Indian question was concerned: "By God, I'm for battle—no peace."

Harney had been on the march for three months, and his men were worn out. When they reached Fort Pierre they must have been completely frustrated by what they found. They undoubtedly had hoped for at least a hot meal and a bunk in a warm barracks. But there was no hot meal; the barracks had no bunks and were ice cold. The nearest wood for heating was twenty miles away. Those men who had to use the latrines found not only that they froze on the trip from the so-called barracks but that an exposed bottom would stick painfully to an icy seat.

Pierre could not accommodate the men who were assigned there, much less the added four companies of dragoons and ten of infantry that came in with Harney. Upon the general's arrival Montgomery was immediately sent away to Fort Leavenworth and dismissed from the army before the end of the year.

Harney took over and tried to make some semblance of order out of the chaotic conditions. First he sent six companies of dragoons and two of infantry upstream about twenty miles where they could find wood to build fires and keep from freezing to death, and even some wood of sufficient size to build log huts to provide shelter during the coming winter. He requisitioned what prefabricated materials he could to build new shelters and to shore up the collapsing buildings at Fort Pierre. He provided for a hot mess and he got the men up off the floor with improvised bunks.

The men who were sent upstream were the lucky ones. They were able to build adequate shelter. Those who stayed behind found that the flimsy, unfinished inner walls were covered with hoar frost. For the most part men left their crude quarters only when absolutely necessary since exposure to the freezing weather for only ten minutes would result in frostbitten faces and hands. They did make it to the mess hall but not too many risked the 250-yard trip to the latrine. Instead, they improvised by cutting holes in the floor. By mid-November the ice on the river was so thick that horses and wagons could cross, and Harney sent two more companies across the river and upstream where they could build huts for the winter. The company tailor had to make fur clothing for those who had to stand duty outside. More than a third of the cavalry horses froze to death, and without fresh fruit and vegetables the men broke out with scurvy; they grew pale and listless, teeth loosened from bloody gums and their flesh became soft.[12]

Harney knew that even those who survived the winter would have a rough time of it in summer, for there was not enough ground suitable for cultivation, and bringing in fresh supplies of food would be too costly and too lengthy an operation. He made plans for a new fort.

Alfred used his free time productively. He did numerous sketches of Fort Pierre and, when the temperature moderated, he did oil paintings of Sioux Indians. The spring after his arrival he sent home three paintings.

119

Sully knew the Indians of Dakota and Minnesota probably better than any other man. And he respected them. They had a dignity that appealed to

him. He wrote that it was beneath this dignity for them to tan hides,
cook, and do other menial tasks reserved for women.

A flat boat has just come down from the Yellowstone River belonging to the American Fur Company and leaves in a few days. On it I send a small box and in the box I have put three pictures. I know sending pictures home is like sending coals to New Castle [sic], but I painted them last winter because I had nothing better to do, and as they are views that I have taken from here, they may interest you. Besides, I have nothing else to do with them and I want father to criticize them and tell me their faults. He need not be afraid of making me feel bad if he has to abuse them very much for I don't consider myself an artist.

The big picture is taken from part of an Indian village when they are dressing buffalo skins. The Indians are the Sioux of this post, and three of them are copied from recollection. The two girls are meant for likenesses. One near the horse is called Peh-han-lota, or Red Crane, the other Ke-me-me-bar, or Butterfly.[13]

Fort Pierre is taken from the ice in the river. Dead buffalo is a common sight during extremely cold winters. The old ones die for want of food and are soon devoured by wolves who always follow in crowds the bands of buffalo. The background of this picture is taken from my window, looking across the river. To fill up the box I also send some moccasins made by the young Dacotah ladies and presented to me by them in the Indian fashion, that is with the idea of getting me to give them something in return. Give them to who ever they will fit.

Alfred did oil paintings of Indians hunting buffalo and breaking camp. Another favorite subject was animals. He was very meticulous in sketching them first, taking great pains to get the proper proportion and position, and in each scene he tried to tell a story. One he called the "Death of the Old King," which shows wolves about to kill an old buffalo. With this one, as with his other oil paintings, he did a number of sketches before starting the finished picture. Even his watercolors were not done until

The Plains Indians did not hunt buffalo for sport. The animal meant food, clothing, and the necessities of life.

When the old buffalo got too old to keep up with the herd, he fell behind and was soon devoured by the wolf pack.

While stationed at Fort Pierre, Alfred devoted a considerable amount of
his free time doing oil paintings of the Indians engaged in their various

activities. Attempts to locate the original of this painting of the encampment of the Yankton Sioux have been in vain.

Fort Dearborn must have been a brief stopping off place for Alfred.
He never mentioned it, and it does not show up in the military records.

he had first drawn the scene the way he wanted it in pencil or pen and ink. He was particularly interested in horses as subjects, and these he usually drew to scale on a graph sheet to make sure his dimensions were accurate.

Wherever he went he took his sketchbook with him. He painted the prairie—afire in winter, and in summer vast sheets of loneliness and emptiness. He visited the forts and he sketched them: Snelling, Ridgely, Randall, Union, Pierre, Kearny, and others.

In June 1856 Harney sent two companies from Alfred's regiment to start construction of Fort Randall. Sully joined them with 114 men in September and helped with the construction. Before the following summer old Fort Pierre had been stripped of all material that could be used to build Randall and was abandoned by the army. A new Fort Pierre was to be built three miles up the river.

The site Harney picked for Fort Randall was on a rise about a half mile from the waterfront on the western side of the Missouri and just north of the Nebraska line. The river at this point was almost 1,000 yards wide and Fort Randall was readily accessible by river boats. It would later serve as Sully's base of operations against the Sioux in 1863, 1864, and 1865. Meanwhile it was from Randall and subsequent forts that Alfred gained the experience that would prompt the secretary of war to select him as the man best qualified to fight what is believed to be the largest number of Indian warriors ever assembled. He would live in hostile Indian country and fight or make peace with more tribes than possibly any other man in the army: the Santee Sioux, Brulé Sioux, Teton Sioux, Winnebagos, Chippewas, Gros-Ventres, Omahas, Poncas, Pawnees, Cheyennes, Rees, Mandans, Crows, and other tribes. He got so that he could think like an Indian.

In 1858, Alfred was sent back to Fort Ridgely. Things were relatively quiet there, and he was granted a leave of absence which enabled him finally to take his trip to Europe. He must have made some connection in Washington, because he was sent as an official "bearer of dispatches" to Madrid, Paris, and Switzerland, with a request from the United States legations in these cities asking "all whom it may concern to permit him to pass freely . . . without molestation . . . and to extend to him such friendly protection as would be extended to citizens and subjects of foreign countries reporting to the United States bearing Dispatches." Surprisingly, however, the trip did not make enough of an impression upon Alfred to cause him to write about it in his letters to Philadelphia.

He got back in time to spend two more years on the frontier fighting the Cheyenne Indians before the outbreak of the Civil War.

Chapter Seven

A Call to War

IN 1861, ALFRED SULLY turned his efforts toward aiding the Northern cause. He was firmly convinced that the North had entered the Civil War in a crusade to save the Union. He realized that the struggle was critical, because there were a number of states as yet undecided in choosing between the North and the South, states that would secede from the Union if the conflict developed into a war to free the slaves.

He had many a long discussion with his friends, both Northerners and Southerners, about the situation. They realized that the angry, lingering suspicions between free states and slave states had been nurtured for several decades, and somewhere there had to come a breaking point. The wealth of the South was built on cotton, and the cotton relied upon Negro labor; the plantation owners had more than three million slaves, and they felt that the North wanted to take away this cheap labor pool. The wealth of the North, on the other hand, was built on industry and farming. The North had its own supply of cheap labor. From 1851 to 1860, more than two and a half million immigrants poured into the United States through Ellis Island[1]—a labor market about equal to the black pool of the South. Irish, Germans, Poles,

Italians, and Scandinavians worked the mills, factories, and fields under conditions that were not much better than those under which the slaves worked, with one exception—the immigrants had their freedom.

Alfred watched the guarded, hostile attitude between the North and the South kept under control until hot-tempered partisans and political opportunists fanned the flame into open conflict. He condemned it bitterly as a power grab by government officials and a money grab by greedy contractors—all people, he said, who would not have to fight. He also felt that the British were involved: "England now has a chance to accomplish her long cherished scheme to humble us, break up a great republic dangerous to all aristocratic institutions. John Bull with all his smooth talk philanthropy about niggers is not the man to let so good a chance slip."

He sympathized with the moral rights and responsibilities of Southern officers who resigned their commissions and joined forces to protect their homes and their families; the goodbyes were said without rancor and usually with a handshake. At the same time he was deeply disturbed by the action of a "Northern officer who accepts office under a foreign flag to fight the flag of his country." He, as much as his country, was torn from within.

The Union had not prepared for the war. The total strength of the army, still scattered across the posts on the western frontier, was less than 16,000 men. Alfred was ordered to Fort Leavenworth to recruit and train 1,000 volunteers from Kansas and Missouri. These two states were seething hotbeds of uncontrolled riots; while neither state had declared its allegiance, they had already started a civil war, brother against brother, within their own state boundaries. And woe betide the outsider who tried to interfere.

Alfred was that outsider. But his years on the frontier had made him indifferent to his own personal safety. By the time he reached Fort Leavenworth, a major at the age of forty-one, he was fatalistic and unafraid. He had the reputation of being a man who would not be crossed, with an ungovernable temper and a flow of profanity that would wither a subordinate or serve as a bible for the most blasphemous trooper. Alfred Sully was ready for his job; and the job was more than ready for him.

Jefferson Davis had been advised that Kansas was controlled by "a poor, worthless, starving bunch of abolitionists who receive their support from donations or provisions from Northern states which are transported through Missouri and delivered to them on the banks of the Missouri River—Missouri cannot be secured to the South unless the country west of it is taken and held by the Confederate States." Fort Leavenworth would be the South's most important objective in Kansas.

The North had recognized the importance and vulnerability of Leavenworth. The place contained large supplies of ordnance —guns, small arms, and equipment—and the troops that were there would have been almost helpless in case of an organized attack upon the post. In addition, there was the still-unresolved question as to which side Kansas would choose.

GENERAL HARNEY ORDERED HIS UNIT to proceed to Leavenworth on April 10, 1861, two days before hostilities broke out at Fort Sumter. They arrived within two weeks. Although Alfred was only a subordinate, he immediately took charge. He sailed up the Missouri to St. Joseph on a recruiting mission, but not before inserting in the newspaper a proclamation to the inhabitants of the town that could have been written by a public relations man:

IMPORTANT PROCLAMATION OF MAJOR SULLY
TO THE INHABITANTS OF ST. JOSEPH
To the Public
Desiring that no apprehension should arise in the public mind in regard to my purpose in taking a military post at

St. Joseph, and to disarm designing men—who are ever ready to misrepresent every movement of my government—of their power of evil, I address a few words to the public. My mission here is one of peace, though prepared I may be to sustain the dignity of my flag, which, I have no doubt, will be sacredly guarded by the patriotic and chivalric people in whose midst I have raised it. Believe me, Missourians, it flaunts no defiance in your face. I am here under orders from our mutual government to execute a peaceful mission, and I sincerely trust that all rumors of hostilities to my encampment are as groundless as I know my purpose to be sincere to preserve the peace and quiet of the community. Every effort upon my part shall be made to effect this object, and no demonstration, individual or by detachment, from my command will be permitted to annoy or in any way interefere with the community in their peaceful avocation. My government makes no war upon your State, and cherishes the hope that she has none to make upon her.

In enrolling volunteers into the United States service, I am obeying orders and but doing what is a recognized right of the United States—a right never yet denied by state authority, and there is now, in the practical exercise of this right on Missouri soil, no cause of irritation or alarm to her citizens. Believe me there is none. I have deemed it proper to give this assurance to my fellow citizens in all candor and to say that I shall make no distinction in my line of conduct. Every citizen, be his political opinions what they may shall be equally respected and his person and property protected should occasion need more than the civil power to do so. In pursuing the line of operations thus marked out, I sincerely hope other parties will give no cause for a departure from them on my part. We can have peace in Missouri if we will, and the true soldier should never needlessly draw his sword.

A. Sully
Commanding United States Forces

131

Whether this proclamation helped or not, the citizens of St. Joseph, who had threatened to blow him out of the water on his arrival, allowed Alfred to go ahead with his work.

He had his hands full. He was responsible for the fortifications and for conducting scouting parties against secessionists. He had to buy horses, break, and drill them. And of course he worked toward his recruitment quota, drilling the new men, organizing a field battery of artillery, and sometimes personally drilling the volunteers (as distinguished from the regular army soldiers) to show their officers how it should be done. He had no regular army officers to help him.

Under these adverse conditions, he wrote optimistically: "I have been enlisting men for the regiments very fast; our ranks are filled [with] as strong [and] healthy looking a set of men as I ever saw. They are all anxious to go East and get into the War. There's some of the greatest dare devil rascals in the ranks you can meet with. If I get to Philadelphia or Washington with them they'll make trouble enough for me to keep them straight."

His pride turned to mortification when Col. Samuel C. Curtis arrived, with one thousand Iowa troops, to take command. Curtis was a strong Republican congressman, and Alfred resented being ordered about by a politician. He particularly objected to having to go to the homes of secessionists at night, seize them, and march them off to jail, "just like a policeman apprehending a thief. I felt like a thief myself. The most disgusting business I ever had to do."

His disagreements with Curtis[2] brought into sharper focus his discontent with the government's system of appointing civilians as officers in the army.

As for myself I am perfectly disgusted with the service and if I had anything else in the world to do would not remain in it one hour to be ranked and commanded by citizens who have not been in the service as many weeks as I have years, or by officers far my juniors whose only reputation in the army has been remarkable for avoiding all duty in the field—nice, good looking, gentlemanly fellows who through political influence have been able to spend all of their time in cities while others have had to do their work, and through that same influence are now put over our heads; and even some of them been made Brigadier Generals. Fremont is a shining example. A bigger humbug never lived. The country will find it out before long at their expense. So far he has done nothing but blunder. He has now issued a proclamation declaring all niggers of secessionists free, giving the rebels a chance of proclaiming that the war is an abolition war and causing hundreds of Union men to secede."

Gen. John C. Frémont had arrived in St. Louis in July 1861, as head of the newly created Western Department, composed of Illinois and states west of the Mississippi. He was supposedly the counterpart of Gen. George B. McClellan, who was commander of the Division of the Potomac in the East. These were the first two top posts filled by President Lincoln in his long and heart-breaking search for a general who could command the Northern armies.

Sully's letter criticizing Frémont was written in mid-September 1861. Before the end of the following month, Frémont had been charged with "neglect of duty, disobedience to orders, gross extravagance, mis-management and mis-application of funds, and of despotic and tyrannical conduct."[3] Lincoln removed him and appointed a regular army officer, Gen. David Hunter, to take his place. At the same time he gave Frémont another, lesser command, but one with an impressive title because Frémont's friends (he was the son-in-law of Senator Thomas Benton) and his political influence were important to the Northern cause. This consideration overshadowed the fact that Frémont had never had even the basic training of a soldier.

Although Missouri was not in the war, there were numerous skirmishes fought between the opposing factions. These were diversions for Alfred.

2.ª BRIGADA DE ARTILLERIA.   COMPAÑIA

REPUBLICA MEGICANA

FILIACION.

March 31st

I am writing this in an old deserted Mexican Apothicary's shop on the Jallapa road. My Company being on picket on this road some 3 or 4 miles from the city (which you know is in our possession)...

A copy of the first page of one of the series of letters Alfred wrote to his sister Blanche, during the early part of his career.

I have been absent on another expedition—got back about two days ago. A large Rebel camp was forming across the river about 20 miles from here. Four companies of a regiment from Nebraska came in on a steamer under the command of Colonel Thayer. Col T——being a militia man and not knowing much about military matters offered me the command and served under me. I took my company, 30 men, two 12-pound guns, which with the Nebraska men made my command 500. Four Italian Officers from Garibaldi's Army who were waiting here for General Lane, being on his staff, begged to accompany me to see how Americans fought. So I got them horses and they accompanied me as a staff. . . . We had a good band of music and made quite a show. Only the staff was so much more splendidly dressed than me, their General, that most of the people I fear took me for an orderly.

We reached the camp after the hottest march I ever experienced, but too late to fire a shot; the enemy had fled in all directions. Hearing that in the City of Independence they had four Union men in jail, I marched there through the town, which is one of the hottest places I have ever seen, the band playing Yankee Doodle and such like tunes. All we saw of the deserters was a cloud of dust their horsemen made in retreat. We forced in part of the jail, took the prisoners out and returned, but not before enjoying a good dinner at the expense of the city. If we did not do much harm, we did some good in scaring the deserters. It is the hottest place I ever saw. How I wish the Rebels would put off their work till the fall.

Alfred enjoyed these brief forays. They helped him to keep his sense of humor, and it was necessary for him to keep active.

THAT NOVEMBER HE GOT HIS ORDERS to report to Washington for more serious involvement in the war. The city was a seething

135

mass of frenzied people—men wanting to get into the army or out of it; people seeking high military commissions or government contracts; soldiers enlisted as volunteers but without orders or quarters; and gamblers, prostitutes, and hangers-on.

While the South had girded itself for a war, the Congress had been content to argue about sugar and coffee rations for the enlisted men and to set up a committee to investigate the curriculum at West Point. This was its sole contribution to military preparedness in 1860.[4] Small wonder it was that on March 4, 1861, President Lincoln, in disguise, had to sneak into the White House with security protection in order to take the oath of office, while Jefferson Davis was calling up a hundred thousand men.[5]

The North had been pushed prematurely into the Battle of Bull Run because the politicians and the press, with the "On to Richmond" slogan, wanted it to look like there would be a quick end to the war. In the battle, on July 21, 1861, the North was soundly defeated. President Lincoln immediately relieved the commanding general, Irvin McDowell.[6] The next day the president was authorized by Congress to raise the strength of the Union Army from 35,000 to more than 500,000 men. These men were quickly formed into militia regiments and poured into Washington before there was any plan for how or where they could be used. They were quartered in the corridors of the Capitol, on the floor of the House—wherever, helter-skelter, they could find shelter.[7] Food, supplies, and sanitary facilities were at best inadequate.

Discipline was nonexistent. Soldiers with no training and no trained leaders refused to obey orders or even to turn out for roll call. They roamed the streets, committing crimes of every sort, and there was no one to apprehend them or even to tell them to stop. Drunkenness and looting were the order of the day. Officers, who only days before had been clerks, bankers, grocers, or druggists with absolutely no military experience, strutted the streets in outlandish uniforms, collected their pay, and stayed away from the troops in self-defense.[8]

Alfred Sully reported with his company to Gen. Andrew Porter, commander of the City Guard, on November 17, 1861. Conditions were no better than they had been when civilians and troops started to pour into the city immediately after the Battle of Bull Run. Alfred wrote:

Office seekers, political plunderers are hard at work to get all they can. Washington to me has always been a disgusting place, a place where broken down speculators come to fill their pockets, and it has not improved since the War. You see and hear very little of the old fashioned patriotism here. Everything is put aside for the almighty dollar. And so it will be until the government is bankrupt.

At the same time Sully was realistic enough to accept the fact that if it took political pull to get anywhere in a situation into which he had been thrust without choice he was going to have to play according to the accepted rules. He was determined never "to take to the field again as a line officer."[9] The years on the open plains had taken their toll; he was bothered by rheumatism, and he did not feel that he could march again under the weather conditions he knew he must face in a winter campaign. So while he was in the capital he made the rounds of the government offices as other officers did.

The lack of discipline galled him, and he was not one to hide his feelings at that point. He was lucky enough to be moved out of Washington soon after his arrival, when he was made provost marshal of Georgetown. But this was still police duty, and he wanted to get into combat. He had to continue to make the rounds of the offices of people with some authority. This took time.

The government was trying to mix regular army men with raw militia, to provide a core of experienced soldiers. At the same time, regular army officers were being passed over for promotions so that local politicians could assume positions of command; the local politicians were needed to attract people and money to the

This Napoleonic pose of Alfred Sully was taken about 1862, at the time his days in the Civil War campaign were ending.

cause of the North, and the regular army officers were not needed because the battles had not really started yet. So a lot of them, like Alfred, sat on their hands. And they made the rounds.

Alfred finally made a contact. He had been friendly with Gen. George B. McClellan, a West Point graduate about six years his junior, and had served with him in Mexico. McClellan had been appointed general in chief of the United States Armies in November 1861, and Alfred wrote that "McClellan and my friends here are disposed to advance me."

George B. McClellan was one of the most controversial figures of the Civil War. He had distinguished himself in the war with Mexico, at Cerro Gordo, Churubusco, Contreras, Veracruz, and Mexico City. He then resigned his commission as a captain to become president of the eastern division of the Ohio and Mississippi Railroad. When the Civil War broke out, he offered his services, was appointed a brigadier general, and was placed in command of the Department of the Ohio, where he was successful in driving the Confederates out of West Virginia. When Lincoln looked for a general to replace McDowell after the fiasco at the First Battle of Bull Run, McClellan was the only one who had had any success in winning battles, even though his "battles" had been minor skirmishes. So McClellan was picked to command the Union forces on the eastern front. He gradually eased out the aged Winfield Scott and became commander in chief of the armies at the tender age of thirty-five.

McClellan was an able administrator. He took the remnants of an army that had been soundly beaten at Bull Run and whipped them into a strong, proud fighting force within a few months. He inspired his men. A dashing figure, full of energy and enthusiasm, he was tremendously popular with everyone—even with Lincoln —but not with the politicians. They felt he might become too powerful.

It was to McClellan that Alfred Sully hitched his star. Even with influence, getting a command position was not easy. Officers for the volunteer regiments were appointed by the state governors. If a governor decided he wanted a particular regular army officer to command one of his regiments, he tendered a commission which first had to be approved by Washington.

Three months after he arrived in Washington, Alfred was offered command of the First Minnesota Volunteer Regiment. "Since that time a cavalry and an infantry regiment have been offered to me, which I declined. They are Pennsylvania troops and maybe it would have been better for me to accept a regiment from my state, but I have been a long time with the Minnesota people and they know me."

McClellan finally got approval for Alfred to accept the commission as a colonel and placed him and his unit under his own command.

Chapter Eight

Harper's Ferry to Fredericksburg

BY THE TIME ALFRED SULLY reached Harper's Ferry in late March 1862, Lincoln had relieved McClellan as general in chief without naming a successor; the president left him in charge of the Army of the Potomac.[1]

McClellan always had great tactics and shrewd strategy to suggest, but he had refused to fight in spite of Lincoln's admonitions that "you must act."[2] Lincoln let McClellan save face by announcing that no man could direct activities from Washington and also lead a force in the field—and Lincoln wanted a man in the field. Almost six months had passed without a battle. He finally forced McClellan to act.

The general had many battle plans, most of which Lincoln felt were impractical. They finally agreed, with some reluctance on the president's part,[3] that McClellan should take his command out of Washington by boat and move down the Potomac to Fortress Monroe. From here his armies would march up the peninsula through Yorktown, Williamsburg, Savage Station, and Seven Pines (Fair Oaks) which would be their base for an attack on Richmond, the capital of the Confederacy. Lincoln still felt that

Alfred Sully mentioned very few people in his Civil War letters. He did dwell on his servant and his horses.

the objective of the Union Army should be to wipe out the Confederate Army, not just to take the ground and hold it. But in spite of his misgivings, he let McClellan go ahead just to get him moving.

Alfred was not aware of the political moves behind the scenes. He still believed in McClellan who, he said, "wisely keeps his own counsel." But he was happy to be in the field. He slept in the rain and tasted the mud. Although he complained about the lack of rations and tents for his men he felt at home to be back in the open again. This time he had an advantage. As a staff officer he could ride. He had his Negro servant Isaiah with him and a new gray Kentucky horse called Possum, in addition to a horse called Bob.

After minor skirmishes with the rebels around Harper's Ferry, he took his command aboard ship and sailed down the river to

Fortress Monroe. It was much more like a picnic than the prelude to a military campaign. Hundreds of boats were strewn out in the harbor and on every one it was just like New Year's Eve.

We arrived here tonight [March 31] about 8. Close by us and all around us for miles are hundreds of lights from as many vessels of all classes; sea steamers, river boats, ships, brigs, schooners, etc., crowded with soldiers, horses, mules, cannon and all parts of an immense army besides men of war. [On] the small steamer I am aboard of, is a crowd of officers, singing, drinking, smoking, while I write this by the light of a drip candle. Two other small steamers contain the rest of my regiment. The men rolled up in their blankets are taking what rest they can on deck, while Bob and Possum tied up with Eva and Isaiah on a pile of hay are enjoying themselves.

We left Alexandria Sunday morning. Last night, owing to a blow, we laid up for the night; but this morning, with a light sun and a calm sea, our fleet of a hundred sail, stretched out over the bay, the bands playing, looking more like a pleasure party than a warlike expedition. I believe all the steamboats of the North are down here. I frequently have seen boats that put me in mind of the North and the Delaware River. Tomorrow we land to march somewheres.

That "somewheres" was Yorktown. This proved to be not a battle, as Alfred hoped, but a siege. McClellan would not attack, and even Alfred was beginning to become a little disenchanted. He had experienced enough fighting to know that you do not win by standing still. Besides, he had worked his men up to fighting edge, and he was afraid they would lose it unless they got into combat soon.

He took advantage of the time to get to know his men better. They were old Minnesota woodsmen, and they built themselves huts to supplement their tent covers of four-by-six-foot pieces of leaky cotton. They cut a road through the woods to Ship's Point at the mouth of the York River, where they got rations, and so had plenty to eat. There were occasional bursts of cannon and rifle fire, and they were close enough to the rebel lines to hear them talk about the "damned Yankees," but neither side launched an offensive.

The Southerners did not want to leave their fortifications, and McClellan was not yet ready to attack. Alfred commented that they were comfortable enough except for the ticks, which his surgeon pulled out each night with his pincers. He observed that he was occupying roughly the same line as the New York troops had occupied during the Revolutionary War, not far from the remains of General Clinton's quarters, "so we are on cherished ground."

The most excitement they had in two or three weeks was when an observation balloon broke loose, and the man in it did not know how to operate the valves. He drifted toward the Confederate side until he finally released the gas so rapidly that he crashed into Sully's camp.

Alfred's letters home showed his impatience: "I will be glad when this siege is over; sieges are always tedious." Word finally drifted down that the siege was not McClellan's idea; the general had wanted to get moving, too. But McClellan had been promised naval support in the form of shelling at Yorktown; he never got it.[4] And at the last minute forty thousand troops under General McDowell had been held back from his command to provide protection for Washington.[5] McClellan delayed and made excuses; his actions were dilatory, not military. After a month he finally decided to move and ordered Sully to take his regiment toward Yorktown.

Alfred found that the enemy had fled. There were no troops behind the fortifications that had been holding up the Union forces.

I marched the First Minnesota with colors flying, over the breast-works and ½ mile down on the road to Yorktown we came in sight of the rear guard of the Rebs, but as they were

mounted and we were not, we entered their Camp, took possession of tents, provisions, arms, etc., etc. A fine house, an old
Virginia home, splendidly furnished, but nobody in it except
an old nigger woman. I placed a guard over it to protect it.
Everything left in confusion.

A great scamp, a Lieutenant of my Regiment from Germany,
opened the piano and played "Hail Columbia", "Yankee
Doodle" and "Dixie", tunes the darned Secests have not
heard for some time.

I write this in the camp of the 14th Alabama in the Colonel's
tent. . . . We reached Yorktown by daylight. A small town, very
old and dilapidated surrounded by a very strong work, in fact
all the works are strong, though I could not visit them; in the
first place not having time, and next as the cowardly rebels have
planted torpedoes all over, whereby several of our men have
been blown up. I slept the first day I entered in the tent of the
Texas Invincibles. Very! All the tents were standing for a great
distance, and even in some the uneaten breakfast. There must
have been at least 7,000 men camped in this one spot. . . . For
the first time I am sleeping on a bed as is a bed. The Rebels
lived better than our troops, judging from their camps. The
Army have pushed on in pursuit. I hope we will follow
tomorrow.

He got his wish in part. On May 11, 1862, he wrote to Blanche
that:

After our taking Yorktown [which I see the abolitionists say
was defended with wooden guns] we pushed on towards
Williamsburg [roughly ten miles west of Yorktown], and after
marching all night in mud up to our knees in the hardest rain I
ever saw, we got orders to return to Yorktown as the battle was
over. We heard all day and part of the night the rattle of musk-
etry. The papers give you an account of it. We lost many more
killed than the rebels, of course, as we had to attack them in a

145

strong position before we got up there and drove them off. We reached Yorktown by Daylight.

We were immediately sent up the York River and reached West Point just as the fight commenced. Here the rebels tried to force us back from the landing, but the troops were landed too rapidly for them.

I got on the field with part of my brigade. Its commanding general being absent, I reported to the commanding general and drew it up as a reserve. But my services were not required. I had to witness the fight as it was ending. We succeeded in driving the rebels back with a loss on our side of about 250. Here again, the woods being very thick where they were and we mostly in open ground, we suffered more than the enemy. The gun boats did us great help by throwing shell into the woods on their flank.

Alfred's troops made camp about three miles beyond West Point. They expected to move on as soon as they received rations, since they were only thirty miles from the Confederate capital. They camped at a Virginia mansion that was older than the Revolution, and there was no one to bother them. All of the inhabitants had fled, "here as every where in Virginia. The papers speak of the Union feeling in the State but I have not seen it. They all look on us as invaders trying to conquer and I believe they hate us as strongly as they can."

Meanwhile, McClellan was in trouble. By the siege of Yorktown the Confederates had gained their objective—a month's delay—and had been able to get provisions and fresh troops. They let McClellan inch closer and closer to Richmond until he was only five miles away. The closer to Richmond he got, the more panicky he became. Typically, he claimed he was greatly outnumbered and screamed for help in every direction he could think of: President Lincoln, Secretary of War Stanton, and Henry W. Halleck, soon to be commander in chief of the armies. He also called on all the forces under his command in the peninsula.

Lincoln promised him McDowell's force of forty thousand men. At the same time, Stanton advised him that McDowell's chief responsibility was the defense of Washington and that McClellan must not issue any orders to McDowell that would interfere with that responsibility: in other words, McClellan had no control over McDowell—it was to be a divided command. Then Washington learned that Stonewall Jackson was on the Potomac in force. McDowell's orders were countermanded, and he was sent to chase Jackson.

In anticipation of reinforcements from McDowell, McClellan left his main force on the north side of the Chickahominy River to move on Richmond from the north, while he kept less than half of his forces on the south side of the river to move up and take the Southern capital in a pincers movement. He was near Fair Oaks, a plantation from which he could strike Richmond with all of his forces in a few hours. But there were no reinforcements in sight on the other side of the river.

Fair Oaks with its pleasant-sounding name was a symbol of gracious living. The people who resided there more than a century ago liked its beauty and serenity—but Civil War buffs remember it as a place where more than ten thousand men wallowed in their own blood, a presage of things to come. Nearby is the Chickahominy River. The rains of late spring and early summer had made an unruly, uncontrollable torrent of the normally placid stream. The bridges were under water and in danger of being swept away at any moment. Seasoned campaigners called the Fair Oaks battle the worst night they had ever seen in combat.

Gen. Joseph E. Johnston, in command of the Confederate forces, felt that McClellan was getting uncomfortably close to Richmond. He also realized that the Union general had only part of his army on the south side of the Chickahominy and that the chances of his getting any help from the other side were slim. He decided the time was ripe to slice McClellan's forces to pieces, and he launched his attack.

147

Alfred hated cowardice, but here he shows compassion for those who were retreating.

By the time Sully's corps arrived, McClellan had convinced himself that the Confederates were concentrating "everything" in front of him, and he was preparing himself for "the last struggle." He needed all the help he could get; Sully had to cross the swollen river. The swaying bridge was moored by ropes tied to stumps upstream and held in place only by the weight of the troops as they crossed. But cross they did.

My regiment being in advance and receiving orders to push on got to the field about 4 p.m. Saturday. Before I reached there I was met by a staff officer who begged us to hurry. All along the road I met wounded being helped to the rear by their all too willing comrades, besides squads of officers and men on their way to the rear.[6] They belonged to Casey's Division,

148

whipped by the Rebels.[7] No entreaty could bring these cowards back. The conduct of Casey's troops was a disgrace to the country. I found on getting on the battlefield the division under General Couch holding their ground manfully. You can't imagine their joy when they saw me filing my regiment out of the woods. General Couch met me, also General Abercrombie whose brigade had been broken to pieces. They begged me to hurry to the right as the Rebels in great force were marching there to get into their rear. We arrived on the battlefield just in time to save our troops already engaged from utter defeat.

Coming out of the woods were thousands of them. They opened fire but I ordered my men to lie down and thereby saved many lives. My regiment had to keep this position for some time alone. I never saw such a hot place. The bullets sang through the leaves just as if a rain storm were taking place, and I can assure you I was rejoiced when other regiments and some artillery were sent to help me. It was now our turn and we drove the enemy with great slaughter. Night closed the scene and we lay down to rest among the dead and wounded. Our wounded were immediately all properly cared for, but the Secests, many of them being in the woods where it was not safe to venture at night, kept me awake all night with their groans.

The next morning, Sunday, the rebels again attacked us in large numbers but were again driven back with more slaughter on both sides. If we could then have got the rest of our army across the Chickahominy, we could have easily have followed them up into Richmond. But the river and roads and rain (it does nothing else in this God forsaken country) stop us and we are giving the Secests time to rally again and give us another battle before our getting into their Capitol. We are now about six miles off; in a straight line four and a half from the top of a tree in my fort (for I have built a fort on my ground) you can see the city. My Negro Isaiah was close by me all the action. Neither of us were touched. A bullet grazed my ear but no harm done. Our loss is severe, over 2,000, the rebels greater. So confident were they of success that pleasure parties were on the field to see the fun. We captured an omnibus with men and women in it on a picnic party.

The Union forces lost over five thousand men at Fair Oaks, and the Confederates an even greater number[8], among them their commanding officer, Gen. Joseph E. Johnston. Robert E. Lee was named to replace him as commander of the Army of Northern Virginia.[9] For his part, Sully was cited for "having turned the tide from defeat to victory," promoted to brevet lieutenant colonel in the regular army, and put in charge of a brigade of about four thousand men, a force normally commanded by a general.[10]

The day after the battle Alfred occupied the "pretty farm house" of Fair Oaks. He cut down all the oaks for a quarter of a mile in front, because he needed a sweeping range for his guns and he also needed the logs as protection for his men. The dead were buried inside the enclosure around the house.

The furniture inside the house was mostly burned on that Saturday night, it being a rainy night, and the house used as a hospital. The wounded were suffering from cold. Of course for the same reason the floors are so colored that no water can remove the stain. Luckily since then the shells that the enemy have from day to day directed against the house have not injured it. I say luckily, for since then I have occupied it as my quarters. I doubt if the owner, Mr. Courtney, will know his house when he sees it, or care to occupy it when he does. Such is war. We are pretty quiet here except for an occasional skirmish . . . we however expect work before long.

Alfred was anxious to get to Richmond. Sometime earlier he had met a Richmond widow named Sophia Webster, about whom his correspondence and his later writings say hardly a thing (perhaps he wanted to keep to himself anything so out of keeping with his tough outer appearance as a new love interest). The story is that she had been Lady Sophia in England with the title, rights, and estates that are usually the heritage of a peeress, but that through some machinations she was sent to America with a governess before she was old enough to claim her inheritance. As a resident of Richmond, Sophia was a Southern sympathizer. When Alfred sent a note to her through the lines that he could "see the lights of Richmond," she sent a reply that he might see the lights of Richmond, but that he would never reach them.

Meanwhile, he was being castigated in the press for destroying Fair Oaks—a charge that did not help his cause with Sophia. With a fury and vituperation that later hardened into a policy of barring newspaper writers from his camps, Alfred plainly told them to sit safely at their little desks while he fought the war. He vehemently told his father that the papers were nothing but a pack of lies and urged him to cancel his subscription to the *Philadelphia Inquirer*. Alfred's attitude did not endear him to the fourth estate. It is probably for this reason that most of his accomplishments from this time forward were relegated to a few lines in the back pages of the newspapers.

Meanwhile, his natural expectation that he would be sent on to Richmond after the victory at Fair Oaks was doomed to disappointment. McClellan, as usual, was slow to move. He always needed more troops, more supplies, better weather. While he could bring an army to fever pitch, he could never bring himself to take them into combat—a vacillation that was to prove his undoing. This weakness was magnified by what he had seen at Fair Oaks; he could never appreciate that soldiers, as soldiers, were expendable, and he could not stand to see men die. When combat was forced upon him he could be found in the rear, planning for the next day. He always felt that he was outnumbered, even though he had numerical superiority. When he complained about the weather, Lincoln commented that the weather was just as bad for the South as it was for the North. He kept urging McClellan to attack, but his general "had the slows."[11] He had the slows so

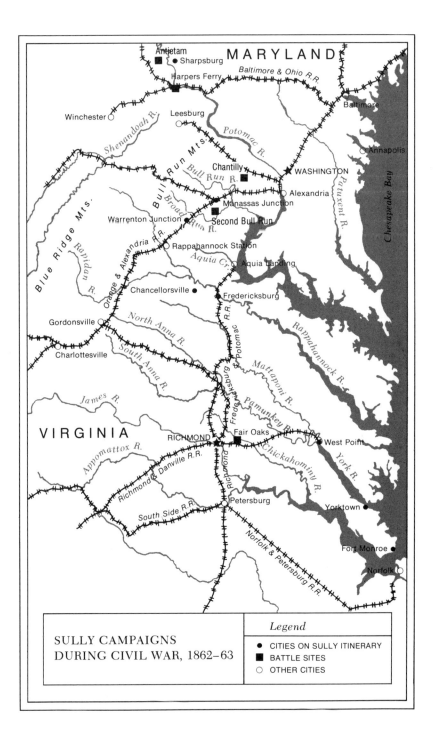

Antietam
■ ● Sharpsburg
Harpers Ferry
MARYLAND
Baltimore & Ohio R.R.
Baltimore
Winchester ○
Leesburg ○
Shenandoah R.
Bull Run Mts.
Potomac R.
Annapolis ○
Chantilly
WASHINGTON
Bull Run R.
Patuxent R.
Chesapeake Bay
Alexandria ○
Manassas Junction
Broad Run R.
Warrenton Junction ●
Second Bull Run ■
Blue Ridge Mts.
Rapidan R.
Orange & Alexandria R.R.
Rappahannock Station ○
Aquia Cr. ○ Aquia Landing
Chancellorsville ●
Fredericksburg ●
Gordonsville ○
North Anna R.
Rappahannock R.
Charlottesville ○
South Anna R.
Fredericksburg & Potomac R.R.
Mattaponi R.
James R.
VIRGINIA
Pamunkey R.
Appomattox R.
RICHMOND ▲
Fair Oaks ■
Chickahominy R.
West Point ●
York R.
Richmond & Danville R.R.
Richmond & Potomac R.R.
Petersburg ○
Yorktown ●
South Side R.R.
Norfolk & Petersburg R.R.
Fort Monroe ●
Norfolk ○

SULLY CAMPAIGNS
DURING CIVIL WAR, 1862–63

Legend
● CITIES ON SULLY ITINERARY
■ BATTLE SITES
○ OTHER CITIES

badly that within a month after the Fair Oaks victory he withdrew down the James River instead of giving chase to the defeated Southerners.

Alfred watched in disbelief while Union guns inflicted 5,000 casualties on the Confederates on July 1, 1862. He knew that over 105,000 Federal troops were available against 85,000 Confederates, that in less than a week the Confederates had suffered 3,478 killed, 16,261 wounded, and 875 missing against Union losses of 1,734 killed, 8,062 wounded, and 6,053 missing. And he knew that when McClellan was again on the verge of success, he withdrew his troops to Harrison's Landing. Yet, he remained loyal to McClellan.

Not so Lincoln. He named Henry W. Halleck general in chief of the armies and commissioned Maj. Gen. John Pope to command the Army of Virginia in place of McClellan. Pope, like his predecessor, had never fought a major battle. He had served in the Mexican War, but his chief military experience had been as a captain of the topographic engineers, where he had spent fourteen years digging artesian wells and served on lighthouse duty for two years before the war. Lincoln was really reaching into the bottom of the barrel.

Pope was anxious to make a name for himself in combat, but he made the mistake of taking on Jackson and Longstreet at the Second Battle of Bull Run, and the only stir he created was the dust raised by his fleeing troops. Alfred Sully was left behind as the rear guard to keep the last of the runners from being butchered. Pope never forgave Sully for saving his hide; Alfred got promoted again, and Pope was transferred to the western front, which was tantamount to being shipped to Siberia.

People who created perplexingly difficult situations were a constant source of annoyance to Alfred Sully. He felt that if a man was wrong in a combat situation, there was no forgiving, no mercy —men's lives were at stake. Yet, he could look at combat situations dispassionately and evaluate the ultimate objective—to win, no matter what the cost.

Alfred loathed Pope almost as much as McClellan did. He regarded Pope as an arrogant, pugnacious popinjay, a bull of a man whose reputation had been built on the false reports he had given to the newspapers about his "glorious" victories in the West, which were sure to end the war in a few days. Where McClellan was overly cautious, Pope was quick on the trigger. He usually acted without listening to the reports or advice of his intelligence officers. He had rushed headlong into the Second Battle of Bull Run with a force of 80,000 men, and of these he lost 14,000 killed, wounded or missing within two weeks—all in a vain attempt to gain personal glory. Lee, who had only 54,000 men lost only 9,000 total casualties.[12] Lee's forces were worn out and poorly supplied, and the ranks were thin. Still, he decided to make a stand at Antietam Creek, even though the odds were against him; McClellan, again in command of the Union forces, had about 90,000 troops while Lee had about half that number. McClellan attacked on September 17, 1862, and there followed one of the most horrible battles of the war. Bruce Catton says of it: "This war saw many terrible battles, and to try to make a ranking of them is just to compare horrors, but it may be that the battle of Antietam was the worst of all. It had, at any rate, the fearful distinction of killing and wounding more Americans in any one day than any other fight in the war."[13] Each side lost close to 13,000 men. Union general "Fighting Joe" Hooker said of it, "Every stalk of corn in the northern and greater part of the field was cut as closely as could have been done with a knife, and the slain lay in rows precisely as they had stood in their ranks a few moments before." The wounded were put into every available shelter: barns, farmhouses, churches, corncribs, the town council room, and the meeting rooms of the Odd Fellows and the Freemasons. The battle was fought by a Dunker church. Though the Dunkers' law decreed that no man who fought in war could be in one of them, the dead, both Blue and Gray, were taken there.[14]

Alfred described the scene: "Yesterday we had a terrible battle. My Regiment lost 147 out of 500. Others nearly in proportion.

The field is filled with dead and wounded. We have the best of it so far. The graves of my own dead and the bad smelling bodies of the Rebels occupy the same ground. For three days we have been hard at work burying the dead Secests and are not quite through. The slaughter has been terrible. I never saw anything like it."

Through all of this, his only personal concern was for the safety of his servant and his horses. Isaiah got "tired" of being shot at and deserted him; his horse got gun-shy, and he planned to put him out to pasture "when he could find one."

He would have a chance to find a pasture sooner than he realized. In disbelief he watched McClellan let Lee's forces cross the river and get away. The Confederates were in sight and within range of McClellan's cannon. But instead of following up his advantage when he had a chance to crush Lee's battered forces, the general chose to withdraw his troops for a rest. Alfred took his brigade to Harper's Ferry.

While McClellan was visiting his wife in Philadelphia and his troops lay idle not far from Lee, the Confederate general was recruiting fresh troops and regrouping. He sent Jeb Stuart and his cavalry to reconnoiter in force. Stuart went up to Chambersburg, Pennsylvania, where they looted the stores of all the food and clothing they could, took Federal uniforms and five hundred horses and paid for everything in Confederate money. Then they boldly rode completely around McClellan's forces and back to their own lines without challenge. Alfred wrote:

We were all surprised yesterday by hearing the rebels, some 2,000, were at Chambersburg, and today they have gone all around us, some 120 miles in 24 hours. I pity their poor horses. They are certainly very daring fellows. I wish I could have time to visit you but don't as yet see any prospect of it. We are too busy and soon must take the field again. While I am writing heavy cannonading is heard in the direction of Poolsville, so I suppose the different bodies of troops sent out here came up with the enemy. Of course we are all anxious to hear the results. Mrs. Montgomery's boy is not the only case where I have been troubled about officers to serve on my Staff. I am only allowed a certain number, and of course want only those who will be of assistance to me. I have no time now to do my duty and teach others their duty.

Lincoln was disturbed by Stuart's ride and said that if it happened again McClellan would be relieved of his command. He was becoming increasingly more impatient. When McClellan pleaded that he needed more horses because his were worn out, Lincoln responded that he had given him every fresh horse he possessed, 7,918, and reminded his general that the army had been inactive for five weeks, and that both horses and men should be sufficiently rested by that time, otherwise, "when could they ever be?" McClellan's repeated requests for more men prompted the ironic remark from the president that since his generals were constantly complaining about being outnumbered three to one or five to one they would need 1,200,000 men in the field instead of the 400,000 they had ready for combat. Lincoln's messages to McClellan to move against the enemy became more urgent and his biting remarks about McClellan's unwillingness to do so became sharper and more frequent.

McClellan began to have visions of the presidency and planned to run for that office. He began to make speeches about how the affairs of the country should be conducted. When Lincoln was asked what he intended to do about this he answered: "Nothing —but it made me think of the man whose horse kicked up and stuck his foot in the stirrup. He said to the horse 'If you are going to get on I will get off.' "[15]

While Lincoln could put up with his subordinate's efforts to unseat him there reached a point in McClellan's military inadequacies beyond which the president could not go. Lee's forces slipped away from the Union Army west to Culpeper. Lincoln promptly replaced McClellan with Gen. Ambrose Burnside on November 7.

It is doubtful if he could have selected a man less qualified for the job. Burnside had graduated from West Point in 1847 and had been among those present at Mexico City. He served on the Mexican Boundary Commission for two years and then resigned from the service in 1853. As a civilian he worked as a cashier for a railroad. When the Civil War broke out he managed to obtain a commission as a colonel of the Rhode Island Volunteers and spent a few months defending Washington. He was not equipped to assume command of a large military force; he knew it and he did not want it. Over his protests Lincoln made him accept the assignment.

By this time Sully was moving his brigade to Warrenton, Virginia, more than half way down between Harper's Ferry and Fredericksburg. On November 10, he prefaced a letter by saying: "fingers so cold can't hold a pen." He wrote:

> We reached this place yesterday, having had a very hard time of it for the last week; sleeping in the mountains in snowstorms without tents and only one blanket each is more than man ought to be expected to live under. Still we were all contented, knowing it would be all right in the end. But an order was received ordering McClellan in the midst of his onward march and victory to leave. They did not want him. It won't be many weeks before they will be begging him to take command as they have twice before. I never saw so universal a feeling of sadness among both officers and men. Burnside is a good General, but he has not the brains of Mac and what is a great deal more he has not by far the confidence of his men. Why this change, many will ask, but anybody acquainted with the corrupt politics of our country can easily see it. I never felt so sad in all my life. Everything before us appears darker than ever. I fear our poor country has not commenced to see the trouble in store. Supposing we should meet again with a defeat, what would be the consequences in the North? I fear a bigger revolution than the present one . . . I wish I had that box with my

overcoat. I am freezing to death.

I have been quite unwell for a few days, but luckily, having a separate command, my Brigade and two batteries to guard the rear, I quartered myself with a well to do Virginia family. They treated me kindly though at first the young ladies did turn up their noses and refuse to come into the room where I was, but this soon wore off and we became quite sociable; the neighbors came in and we lived quite happy. They were not to blame as they lost their only brother in the last fight.

By November 19 he had moved his camp to Falmouth in the vicinity of Fredericksburg.

A rapid march brought us from Warrenton to this place day before yesterday. On our approach the enemy fired at us from across the river. Our artillery being ordered ahead, a short duel of shells at long range soon quieted them without any serious results. They still are in sight across the river but neither of us fire. Falmouth as you know is on the north side of the Rappahannock. Fredericksburg is opposite. As the Rebs have destroyed the bridges some few days must pass before we can find means to cross. Where we will go to when we cross I can't say. I don't think much of the plan to march south by land. It is raining now; a few days may make the roads impassable. McClellan's plan was the best. Had he not been relieved, in two days we would have been at Culpeper and then cut the retreating army in two. A battle with their divided forces could not fail to have been successful. There is a great depression in the spirit of officers and men at his removal. Whatever the world may say of him, he certainly had the hearts of the Old Army of the Potomac with him, and they would have willingly followed him wherever he might direct. But as a soldier of course I must obey orders and I shall act as I have always, do my duty and try not to grumble. I very much fear however this war may turn to a pure abolition war. I hope not, for I don't know how I shall act or what to do. I am fighting for one thing: my country, our old flag, but have my own ideas of liberating the slaves.

In viewing Fredericksburg as a battlefield, Alfred saw that the situation was impossible for the attacking force. The town nestled innocently enough by the side of a river. Across the river was a long peaceful stretch of open field, which ran to a stone wall that kept a dirt road from washing away. But beyond the dirt road and for half a mile or more was an almost insurmountable hill which reached toward the sky—to heaven or hell, depending upon which side you were on—at an unbelievable forty-five-degree angle. He felt that it was plain suicide to cross the streets of the town, to attempt to cross the river, or to claw your way up the open field and try to cross the stone wall; but most of all it was certain death to climb the hill on the other side of the stone wall.

The town itself was deserted.

We had a terrible fight and with no good result except the taking of a city which we had to knock to pieces with our guns and which did not contain 25 persons. As we landed late the enemy fought us in the streets killing many of our men; the place was sacked. The soldiers, breaking into the liquor stores, got drunk and all in all it was a frightful scene. On Saturday we tried to take the hills behind, but it is fortified so strongly that we could not, though most of our troops behaved magnificently. Oh that McClellan were here. I am stopping in a magnificent house, splendidly furnished but riddled with cannon balls, but few rooms having escaped.

The hills were impossible to take. Lee was well entrenched on the top of Marye's Hill, with 72,000 men and cannon waiting for Burnside's force of 113,000 to cross the river and try to come up to him.[15] When the firing began, 2,000 men were killed in a matter of minutes. Alfred's force made fourteen frontal assaults. He never got within one hundred yards of the road at the base of the hill where the Confederate forces had their cannon; no Union soldier got any closer than that during the entire battle. The Union Army lost more than 12,500 men [more than they had lost at Antietam] and the Confederates more than 5,000.[16] Eventually Burnside's generals convinced him that the attack was hopeless, and he retired into military limbo.

Characteristically, Alfred took time to assure his family that he was not wounded. He was never wounded in combat, although he was emotionally exhausted and physically ill. "To show you how well I am, I am placed in command of the 3rd Division, 2nd Corps, Army of the Potomac. So direct your letters in future. It is the Command of a Major General of 10,000 men, but I have not *political* influence enough to give me the rank and pay. Most of my troops are very green and new, and I can assure you I have work enough to get them in trim."

Alfred, however, was not destined to take these troops into combat. He was needed elsewhere. He had been in every battle in the peninsula campaign: Antietam, Savage Station, Glendale, Malvern Hill, Yorktown, West Point, Bull Run, Peach Orchard, Fredericksburg, Chancellorsville, Fair Oaks, and the others. His promotions after these battles were frequent: He rose from captain to general in less than six months on merit alone, in spite of the fact that he had no political connection. There was a war still to be won in the East, and he wanted to stay on until the end.

But there was an Indian uprising in the Northwest serious enough to make it possible that the Union would have to open a new fighting front and thus drain off troops needed to finish the Civil War. Alfred was ordered to return to Minnesota and the Dakotas to stop the uprising and drive the Indians back. He was not happy about the assignment, particularly because it meant he would be reporting to Gen. John Pope.

As he left for the frontier, Alfred Sully was an embittered, disillusioned man. At the age of forty-three, he looked sixty. He had watched five generals fall—McDowell and Scott, McClellan, Pope, and Burnside—all in a year and a half. He had been in the toughest battles of the war, those where most of the men were getting killed, and he had rarely tasted the sweet, heady glow of victory—only the bitterness of defeat brought on by incompetent leaders.

But in spite of his brilliant war record it was in Minnesota and the Dakotas that Alfred was to make his greatest contribution to his country's welfare. It was here that he was to gain his reputation as one of the country's greatest Indian fighters.

Chapter Nine

The Great Sioux Uprising

ONCE THE CIVIL WAR HAD BROKEN OUT, the Union left few seasoned troops in the Northwest. And as those few needed replacements, Washington could ill afford to send out tough, combathardened men, further decimating units whose strength had already been depleted by casualties. So the guarding of the frontier was left to citizens and raw militia.

But the great Sioux uprising of 1862 forced the Union to reexamine its policy. The causes of Sioux unrest were many: The whites encroached on their hunting and fishing grounds. Indian agents were holding back goods that were to be given to the Indians, and many agents became wealthy on salaries of $1,500 a year—their politically inspired appointments amounted to a license to steal.[1] Traders who overcharged the Indians for goods bought on credit regularly stood beside the pay tables when the annuities were given out and took their blood money before the Indians even saw it. Both annuities and goods, promised by treaty in 1858,[2] were slow in coming, and the Indians began to resent the fact that under the terms of this treaty the Yankton Sioux had given away fourteen million acres of land between the Big Sioux and the Upper Missouri rivers and had nothing to show for it. The majority of the Indians were opposed to the whites' illegal traffic in liquor—the wild tribes would have nothing to do with it. Finally, there was violent opposition to the government's policy of withholding annuities in repayment for damages alleged to have been caused by Indians.

Their resentment gradually turned to anger. Sporadically, small Indian raiding parties would kill a few whites. The tough Minnesota families accepted this as a way of life. They were generally friendly with the Indians, joined with them in shooting matches, took them into their homes, and fed them when the Indians were hungry and came begging to their doors.

The situation came to a head in August 1862. The coffee, sugar, flour, lard, pork, and other provisions had not been issued, and winter was coming on; the Indians were mindful of the fact that the previous winter a crop failure had caused them great suffering for lack of food.

These conditions, combined with encouragement from the British and the knowledge that the United States Army was occupied elsewhere, caused the Indians to forget their individual tribal squabbles and band together in a formidable fighting force. On July 14, 1862, four thousand of them who were entitled to annuities and another thousand who were not, showed up at the Upper Yankton agency, about forty miles northwest of Fort Ridgely, and demanded payment. The goods were there, but the agent, Thomas J. Galbraith, was reluctant to yield to their demands because he was waiting for the annuity money to come in. He wanted to distribute both the money and the goods at the same time; moreover, he felt that to accede to their demands might be a show of weakness. But the Indians could see the stocked storehouses, and five thousand angry Indians were a pretty persuasive argument; Galbraith made a partial distribution of the goods.

The Indians were not satisfied with what they got and worked their way south along the river, raiding every house as they went. They killed 757 whites, many of them farmers, shop-keepers, and their families. A forty-eight man relief force was sent to the rescue, but half of them were killed.[3] Refugees began to pour into Fort Ridgely. Two hundred and fifty of them were there when the Indians attacked on August 20.

Although Alfred had helped to build Ridgely as an infantry fort nearly a decade before, there were a few pieces of ancient artil-lery left for show. Fortunately, the handful of artillery men sta-tioned there kept these in working condition. When the Indians got to the fort, these men maneuvered the old cannon into firing position, loaded it with grapeshot, chain, stone, and whatever else happened to be lying around loose, and fired point-blank into the Indians who were charging the fort. The Indians were not accustomed to cannon fire, and their losses were severe. They withdrew to think it over.

In a few days they tried again. They threw torches into the barn and set it on fire. Then they went in. At this point the sutler's wife opened the barn door and Sgt. John Jones, the artilleryman, fired through one end of the barn and out the other. Scores of Indians were killed, and those who survived were routed.[4] They decided that cannon was not for them. Besides, the supplies of goods and food at the fort were not as plentiful as they were at New Ulm, about fifteen miles downstream on the other side of the river, so they headed there.

New Ulm was one of the most prosperous and fastest-growing towns on the frontier, with numerous stores, two good hotels, and a population of 900 people, mostly Germans.[5] It is estimated that between 500 and 800 warriors attacked New Ulm. Judge Charles E. Flandrau was elected to lead the defense of the town. He built a barricade, behind which all citizens gathered, and burned the houses on the other side of town so that the Indians could not use them for shelter. When the Indians attacked, they killed ten men and wounded fifty more in the first hour. That night Flandrau had all of the remaining buildings in town set afire, and the town

164

was evacuated. The "Minnesota Massacre" became front-page news, even with the Civil War battles still helping to sell newspapers.

Minnesota people were pretty stolid, but the massacre put them in a state of panic. Indian raids had caused more than a quarter of the estimated 147,000 people in the state to desert their homes and belongings. Most of them fled into Iowa, and many never came back.[6] Heavy pressure was brought to bear upon Washington by both the settlers and the many land companies doing business in the area to get troops there to protect them—and to protect the Union from having to fight a new war on another front.

But the War Department insisted that Minnesotans would have to rely on a hastily-assembled militia, the greenest of men from all walks of life, most of whom did not even have weapons more deadly than pitchforks. The government agreed to provide some seasoned combat officers to train and lead them. Unfortunately for the officers who would have to lead this motley band, the War Department added some "Galvanized Yankees," or Southern prisoners on parole as long as they did not have to fight against the South. They did not take kindly to Yankee commanders. It was an unruly mixture for the core of a fighting force—good fighting men who were sullen and contemptuous of their leaders and men who were untried and ill-equipped. This was to be the nucleus of Alfred's command.

To get rid of Pope after his stinging defeat at Bull Run, Lincoln had created the Department of the Northwest and sent the general there. Pope bitterly resented the rebuke. He immediately initiated a furtive move to get out. The massacre in Minnesota had occurred in August. By the time Pope arrived to take command in September, Col. Henry H. Sibley had an army of over 1,400 militia in the field. Late that month, this force met and defeated the main body of the Sioux bands at the Yellow Medicine River, but most of the warriors and their chief escaped into British territory where they were given sanctuary.[7] In his communications to Sibley, Pope referred to the fight as a skirmish; but in his letters to Henry W. Halleck, general in chief of the armies, he referred to it as the end of the Sioux War. In order to get back east, Pope had Sibley promoted to brigadier general and placed in a position where he could take over for Pope. But he soon found that the Sioux Wars were far from over, and he resigned himself to making plans for a campaign in the spring of 1863.

In planning his campaign, Pope seems either to have recognized that he was not competent to take troops into combat or simply to have wanted to be the man who pulled the strings. His first move was to request that one of his former staff officers, Gen. C. W. Roberts, be assigned to him to lead the field expedition against the Sioux. General Halleck agreed, and Roberts was ordered to report to Pope.

As for Roberts, the secretary of war, Edwin M. Stanton, felt that his only qualification was that he was a friend of Pope's. He countermanded Halleck's order. Before Roberts arrived in Sioux City, Halleck wired Pope: "I think you will do wrong to send Roberts in charge of the Missouri Expedition. Sully is the man for that place. . . . Secretary [Stanton] directed me to say to you that Roberts should not be assigned as you propose."[8]

When Sully arrived in Sioux City to take command, he was under an officer who not only bitterly resented having him there but who was suspicious of his connections in the War Department. Pope whined that they had sent him an officer who was too old (forty-three), too sick (suffering from rheumatism and malaria), and too drunk to take the field. But Alfred assumed command of the expedition anyway, reporting directly to Pope.

One of the most popular men in Minnesota was Henry Hastings Sibley. In 1834, he had come to Mendota, near Fort Snelling, with the American Fur Company; in five years he was made a partner. He had a law degree from Michigan and was a liberally educated man, an avid reader of the classics. He quar-

ried limestone and built a house for entertaining; the down-
stairs was for the elite, but there was an open room upstairs
(entered from the outside) for any Indians who wanted to bed
down. The front of his house was used as a storeroom.

In his first year there he shipped 389,000 muskrat skins, 3,000
mink pelts, 3,000 deer skins, 2,000 racoons, and 1,000 each of
otter and buffalo, as well as beaver, martin, bear, fox, badger,
wildcat, and rabbit.[9] Sibley loved to hunt, and he spent a great
deal of time with the Indians. He was as popular with the
intelligentsia as he was with the backwoodsmen; he was also
extremely popular with the ladies. He became the state's first
elected governor.

In Sibley Pope saw his chance to discredit Sully. And he had
a plan: the Sioux were on both sides of the Missouri; let Sibley,
who like most generals on the Union side had never fought a
major battle, parade a force up the river on the east side and
frighten the Indians into crossing the Missouri; then let Sully
have the responsibility of destroying the Indians on the west
side, even if it meant he had to follow them all the way to the
Yellowstone River. Pope must have felt that no man could
accomplish this mission under the conditions he set down, and
he planned to harass his new general at every possible turn.

It is not difficult to imagine what Alfred's feelings must have
been when the haughty Pope issued his combat orders. Sibley
had a force of 2,000 infantry, 800 cavalry, and several howitzer
batteries. Sully, on the other hand, was to recruit and train his
army in three weeks, see that they were equipped, and have
them ready to march and fight. The two forces were to meet at
Fort Pierre, about six hundred miles to the north, on July 25,
1863. Pope was convinced that the Indians were near there at
Devils Lake.

Sibley marched out in a glory train with a column five miles
long. Undaunted, Alfred went about getting troops. As a start
he had his "galvanized Yankees" and citizen soldiers; then he
got some troops from the Forty-first Iowa Infantry, a detachment

from the Thirtieth Wisconsin Infantry, two companies of Dakota Cavalry, one company from the Seventh Iowa Cavalry, and eight companies from the Second Nebraska Cavalry.[10] He supplemented these troops with what men he could recruit in the area. It was a respectable force in terms of numbers, but they had never drilled together nor marched together, much less fought together. In fact, a great number of them had never done any of these things on their own or in small detachments. And there was no time to teach them.

Sibley's column was meant to impress the Indians, but it did not impress the settlers. Just after the start of the uprisings the previous summer, and while he was on the march to relieve New Ulm, Sibley had taken four days for what was normally a march of one day; he stopped off for a day to "treat the command to a dress parade."[11] The *St. Cloud Democrat* dubbed him "the state undertaker with his company of gravediggers";[12] the *Hastings Independent* called him "a snail who falls back on his authority and assumed dignity and refuses to march." Sheriff Roos of New Ulm begged the governor, "Send us an earnest young man to take command. Such a man will do more with the present force than Sibley ever would do with ten or fifteen thousand troops. He is, in my mind, a coward."[13]

The Indians laughed at Sibley's slow movements, thinking his failure to move ahead was absolutely incredible. They concluded that white people must not care much about their wives and children. At the same time, Sibley was raising the same old cry that all losers in the army voiced: bad weather, bad roads, and the need for still more men and more supplies.[14]

Sully started out from the vicinity of Fort Ridgely on June 20, 1863, three weeks after he had assumed command at Sioux City.[15] The people were not enthusiastic about his chances for success, either. Pope's orders made him dependent upon riverboats for his rations, and this tied his force to the river, leaving him little leeway to maneuver. Moreover, the river was too low to let boats get far upstream. Rainfall and snow had been light

168

that year, and drought conditions existed. The grass had burned to a crisp; the river beds had dried up, and the heat and dust made long marches unbearable, indeed all but impossible. But Sully reached Fort Pierre on July 25, the day designated by Pope for him to combine forces with Sibley.

Sibley did not show up. He had had a few minor skirmishes with the Indians, watched them cross to the west side of the Missouri, and then returned to his home base. Friendly Indians advised Alfred that the warriors had recrossed the Missouri as soon as Sibley left.

Alfred waited for his supply boats. He was visited by the Winnebagos, who begged him to intercede for them. Their reservation land was poor, and dry because of inadequate rainfall; they were being chastized by their neighbors, the Sioux; finally, they no longer had hunting grounds. Alfred did intercede for them, but there is no record that his pleas on their behalf were heard.

On August 14, after a three-week delay, the boat *Alone* arrived with some of his supplies—not all he needed, but enough to get him started again. He left word for the next boat to meet him at the mouth of the Little Cheyenne River. The *Belle Peoria* arrived there three days after he did, and Sully started out after the Sioux.

Meanwhile Pope was writing nasty letters to both Sully and Halleck. To Halleck he wrote: "General Sully has not made the progress expected of him and which it was in his power to have made, but the Indians were so badly worsted by Sibley and are in so destitute a condition that he has nothing to do except follow up Sibley's success with ordinary energy and the whole of the Indians on the Upper Missouri will be reduced to a state of quiet which has not been obtained for years."[16]

To Sully he wrote: "It is painful for me to find fault, nor do I desire to say what is unpleasant, but I feel bound to tell you frankly that your movements have greatly disappointed me, and I can find no satisfactory explanation of them."[17] He ordered

Alfred to return immediately to the Missouri and conduct small raids from there until the onset of winter.

Whether Pope's orders arrived too late or whether Alfred decided to disobey orders and follow his instincts will probably never be ascertained. At any rate, Alfred proceeded after the Indians as soon as he had supplies. He shipped all the baggage of the officers and men back on the riverboat to Fort Pierre, sent back all those men not combat-ready, and transferred all his supplies—about twenty-three days of rations and forage—to mule teams. Before he could get started, he was "visited by one of the most terrific rain and hail storms I have ever seen." His animals stampeded. Some of the mules drowned trying to swim across the Missouri, and he lost a considerable amount of rations.

Nevertheless, on August 21 he started.

On the 24th we marched due north eighteen miles and encamped on a small creek called Bois Cache. Here we came into the buffalo country and I formed a hunting party for the command which I had soon to disband as they disabled more horses than buffalo. . . . Early on the morning of the 26th I sent out a small scouting party, who captured two squaws and some children and brought them into me. These Indians reported that General Sibley had had a fight near the head of Long Lake and that they were on their way to the Agency at Crow Creek, but were lost, and were alone; but the scouts found tracks of lodges going up the Missouri.

I therefor immediately detailed companies F and K of the 2nd Nebraska cavalry under the command of Captain La Boo, ordering them to go to the Missouri and follow up the trail with orders to capture some Indians, if possible, and bring them in so that I might get information; if they could not do that to kill them and destroy their camp. I continued the march with the rest of the command that day, passing through large herds of buffalo and was obliged to make a march of thirty five miles before I could reach water. The weather was very hot and it was night before we reached camp on the Beaver River.[18]

Along the march he found an Indian who had the reputation of being "a good Indian," and from him he learned of Sibley's movements. He was also told that the Indians following Sibley back south had come across

a Mackinaw boat on its way down. They attacked the boat, fought the entire day until sundown, sank her and killed all on board—twenty one men, three women and some children; that before she was sunk the fire from the boat killed ninety one Indians and wounded many more; that a small war party followed Sibley some days, and returned with the report that he had crossed the James River; then some of the Indians went north; the larger portion however went towards the head of Long Lake, and that he thought a portion of them were encamped on the Missouri west of me.

This report was so much in keeping with the Indian mode of warfare that though it came from an Indian I was led to give it some consideration particularly the part that stated the Indians, after watching Sibley's return, recrossed when all danger was over, and went back to their old hunting grounds. Besides, the guides who were acquainted with the country stated that "a large body of Indians could not live long on the other side without going a great distance west; always at this season of the year the Indians camped on the Coteau, near the tributaries of the James where the numerous lakes or springs kept the grass fresh; here the buffalo were plenty and the lakes and streams full of fish; and here they prepared their meat for the winter moving to the Missouri where the fuel was plenty to winter." I therefore determined to change my course towards the east, to move rapidly and go as far as my rations would allow. . . .

171

*Francois La Framboise acted as the half-breed
guide for Major House.*

On the 3rd of September we reached a lake, where on the
plains nearby, were the remains of a very large number of
buffalo killed, some quite recently. Here I encamped to await
reports of the commands I had out during the march, who
every day discovered fresh signs of Indians, their lodges
spread over the country, but all moving towards a point
known to be a favorite haunt of the Indians. I had this day
detailed one battalion of the 6th Iowa, Major House Commanding, and Mr. Frank La Fromboise as guide to keep
ahead of me five miles and in case they saw a small band of
Indians to attack them or take them prisoners. In case they
should find a large band, too large to successfully cope with,
to watch the camp at a distance, and send back word to me,

my intention being to leave my train under the charge of a heavy guard, move up in the night time so as to surround them, and to attack them at daybreak. But for some reason satisfactory to the guide, he bore off much to my left, and came upon the Indians in an encampment of over four hundred lodges, some say six hundred, in ravines, where they felt perfectly secure, being fully persuaded that I was still on my way up the Missouri. This is what the Indian prisoners say. They also state that a war party followed me on my way up in hopes of stampeding me; but this they could not do. I marched with great care, with advance guard and flankers; the train in two lines sixty paces apart; the troops on each side; in front and center myself with one company and the battery; all the loose stock was kept between the lines of wagons. In this way I lost no animals on the campaign except some few, about a dozen, that got out of the camp at night. Nor did the Indians during the trip, ever attack me or try to stampede me.

Major House, according to my instructions, endeavored to surround and keep in the Indians until word could be sent to me; but this was an impossibility with his 33 men, and the encampment was very large, mustering at least 1,200 warriors. This is what the Indians say they had; but I, as well as everybody in the command say 1,500. These Indians were partly Santees from Minnesota; Cutheads from the Coteau, Yanktonais and some Blackfeet who belong to the other side of the Missouri, and, as I have since learned, Unkpapas, the same party who fought General Sibley and destroyed the Mackinaw boat. Of this I have unmistakeable proof from letters and papers found in the camp and on the persons of some of the Indians, besides relics of the late Minnesota massacre; also from the fact that they told Mr. La Fromboise, the guide, when he was surrounded by about 200 of them, that "they had fought General Sibley and they could not see why the whites wanted to come and fight them unless they were tired of living and wanted to die."

Mr. La Fromboise succeeded in getting away from them after some difficulty and ran his horse a distance of more than ten miles in order to give me information, Major House with his command still remaining there. He reached me a little after four o'clock. I immediately turned out my command. The horses at the time were grazing. At the sound of the bugle the men rushed with a cheer, and in a very few minutes saddled up and were in line. I left four companies and all of the men who were poorly mounted in the camp, with orders to strike the tents and corral the wagons, and starting off with the 2nd Nebraska on the right, the 6th Iowa on the left, one company of the 7th Iowa and the battery in the centre, at a full gallop, we made the distance of over ten miles in much less than an hour.

On reaching the ground I found that the enemy were leaving and carrying off what plunder they could. Many lodges, however, were still standing. I ordered Colonel Furnas, 2nd Nebraska to push his horse to the utmost so as to reach the camp and assist Major House in keeping the Indians corraled. This order was obeyed with great alacrity, the regiment going over the plains at a full run. I was close upon the rear of the regiment with the Sixth Iowa. The Nebraska took to the right of the camp and was soon lost in a cloud of dust over the hills. I ordered Colonel Wilson, Sixth Iowa, to take the left, while I with the battery, one company of the Seventh Iowa, Captain Millard, and two companies of the Sixth Iowa, Major Ten Broeck commanding, charged through the centre of the encampment.

I here found an Indian chief by the name of Little Soldier with some of his followers about him. This Indian always had the reputation of being a "good Indian" and friendly. I placed them under guard and moved on. Shortly after I met with the notorious chief Big Head and some of his men. They were dressed for a fight but my men cut them off. These Indians, together with some of their warriors, mustering about 30, together with squaws, children, ponies and dogs gave themselves up, numbering about 120 human beings.

About the same time firing began about half a mile from me ahead and was kept up becoming more and more brisk until it was quite a respectable engagement. A report was brought to me (which proved to be false) that the Indians were driving back some of my command. I immediately took possession of the hillocks nearby, forming line and placing the battery in the centre on a high knoll. At this time night had set in but still the engagement was briskly kept up and in the melee it was hard to distinguish my line from that of the enemy. The Indians made a very desperate resistance, but finally broke and fled pursued in every direction by bodies of my troops.

I would here state that the troops though mounted were armed with rifles and, according to my orders, most of them dismounted and fought afoot until the enemy broke, when they remounted and went in pursuit. It is to be regretted that I could not have had an hour or two more of daylight, for I feel sure that if I had I could have annihilated the enemy. As it was I believe I can safely say I gave them one of the most severe punishments that the Indians have ever received.[19] After night set in the engagement was of such a ... nature that it was hard to tell what result would happen. I therefor ordered all the buglers to sound the "rally" and building large fires remained under arms during the night collecting together my troops.

The next morning early [the 4th] I established my camp on the battlefield, the wagon train under charge of Major Gorman having for the night been ordered to join me, and sent out strong scouting parties in different directions to scour the country and overtake what Indians they could, but in this they were not very successful though some of them had some little skirmishes. They found the dead and wounded in all directions, some miles from the battlefield; also immense

At White Stone Hill on September 3, 1863, Sully decisively defeated fifteen hundred Sioux warriors and burned up "over four or five

hundred pounds of dried buffalo meat," and other items of food, clothing, and shelter they needed for survival.

quantities of provisions, baggage, etc., where they apparently cut loose their ponies from "travailles" and got all on them; also large numbers of ponies and dogs harnessed to "travailles" running all over the prairie. The party that I sent out went to the James River and found there eleven dead Indians. The deserted camp of the Indians together with the country all around was covered with their plunder. I devoted this day together with the following [the 5th] to destroying this property still scouring the country.

I do not think I exaggerate in the least when I say that I burned up over four or five hundred thousand pounds of dried buffalo meat as one item besides the hundred lodges and a very large quantity of property of great value to the Indians. A very large number of ponies were found dead and wounded on the field and besides a large number were captured. By actual count the number of my prisoners is 156 men —32 women and children. I would also beg to say that in the action I had of my command between 600 and 700 men actually engaged. My killed numbered as far as I can ascertain: killed 20, wounded 38.

Although Alfred had acted without Pope's approval, Pope was elated at the victory. He even sent a semblance of an apology for his past behavior and asked Alfred to take measures to ensure his comfort and good health. Since Sibley had fizzled out, Pope needed a winner to make him look good. On October 5, 1863, he wrote to Sully: "I have no purpose to keep you personally in that region this winter but as soon as your troops are posted and supplied and everything is in train to go on smoothly for the winter, I hope you will come down here [Milwaukee], and I will do everything in my power to accommodate your wishes for the winter.[20]

"I trust you will believe my feelings toward you are of the friendliest character, and that nothing I can do shall be wanting which can promote your interests or your pleasure."[21]

He also wrote: "Whilst I regret that difficulties and obstacles of a serious character prevented your cooperation with General Sibley at the time hoped, I bear willing testimony to the distinguished conduct of yourself and your command and to the important service you have rendered to yourself and to the Government—to yourself and your command, I tender my thanks and congratulations."[22]

This squirming must indeed have been music to Alfred's ears, but he did not accept Pope's invitation to winter with him, in spite of the promises of luxury living. He was not quite as jubilant as Pope over the results of the Battle of White Stone Hill. He would not be satisfied until the Sioux were completely destroyed as a fighting force or until they were driven so far from that section of the country that they could not return to Minnesota or Dakota Territory. He wrote no glowing reports that the wars in the Dakotas, Minnesota, and the areas around the Missouri were over. Instead, even as some settlers returned to their farms, he warned the people that poverty would drive together the Indians. Tribes that had long fought each other were going to band together—the Sioux, Cheyenne, Blackfeet, Arapaho, and lesser fighters. He predicted that they would rob or kill to get food during the winter, and that once spring came and the forage was high enough, they would be back to strike again. Alfred made his own battle plans for the spring of 1864.

Chapter Ten

Battle of the Bad Lands

SULLY WANTED TO START EARLY in the spring. When he asked
Pope in February for reinforcements, Pope replied: "Whether I
will be able to get you eight or nine companies of cavalry I do not
yet know. Will at least get you one battalion of the Seventh Iowa
in addition to the battalion now with your two hundred scouts. If
we can get no more you must do the best you can with these."[1]

Once assembled, Sully's army came to 4,000 cavalry, 800
mounted infantry, twelve pieces of artillery (six-pound smooth
bores and twelve-pound mountain howitzers), 300 wagon teams,
a herd of 300 beef steers, and 15 Missouri River steamboats to
carry his supplies north. This time he had seasoned men, but they
were from units that had been broken up into small detachments
for frontier duty, their present units dating only from the Minnesota Massacres. Also, they were mounted for the first time, and
this presented some difficulties.

The government had provided small Canadian ponies[2] rather
than the stronger army horses, because it was felt that the ponies
would be faster and more readily adaptable to the demands of an
expedition of this kind. But the ponies were green, the infantry-

180

men were big, and they carried knapsacks, blankets, haversacks, rifles, and horse equipment. Fortunately, they drilled on the open prairie. When they first mounted as units, men were thrown, ponies ran free, and equipment was strewn all over the field. Gradually, however, men and horses got to know each other. They redistributed the loads, and the ponies got used to the weight.[3]

The question of supplies continued to plague Alfred. On April 25, 1864, he wrote to the quartermaster in St. Louis:

I have to protest in the strongest terms against the unnecessary delay in the transporting of stores to Sioux City required by my expedition. Today I met Captain Ford of St. Joseph who was in charge of shipping these stores from St. Joseph up the river. To my utter astonishment he informed me that all the stores shipped from here [St. Louis] are in storehouses in St. Joseph or are on the road. That he intended to ship the first steamboat load to Sioux City one week from today, that is on the 2nd of May. With good luck it may reach them about the 8th, and that he intends to ship one load every second week, till it all reached them. Thus these supplies required to start the troops in the field cannot possibly all reach Sioux City before the 1st of June. I therefor could not reach Long Lake till July after river had fallen in that section and the expedition will be a perfect failure. . . . In addition to this I would beg leave to inform you that I have a Battalion of men just mustered in without a blanket or tent, and that the supply of rations will be out at Sioux City by May 1st.

He had been glad that he was not committed to rendezvous with another force on the expedition, but he met with another encumbrance. When it was known that he was headed for Yellowstone country, an emigrant train of 123 wagons and about 250 people attached itself to him. Alfred was furious. He publicly told them that emigrants who could not fight had no place in a combat mission—they would hold him back from accomplishing his

181

Indian expeditions in the early 1860s were dependent on steamboats for supplies. This limited their operations to within striking distance of

the rivers. The waters were not always navigable, and many
boats were lost to the elements or to Indian raiding parties.

assignment. The march into territory where no white man had ever been was extremely dangerous and difficult, and they might not survive. Besides, he felt that all able-bodied male emigrants were moving west to avoid military service. But they stubbornly insisted on accompanying him, and under orders and duress he had to offer them protection, much as he knew that they would slow him down, have trouble with their wagons, and try to tell him how to run the train. There would be merchants, lawyers, farmers, and hangers-on, but no fighters.

Sully did not get his column under way until July 4. The start was difficult. His supply officer had failed to provide saddle blankets for the mules, so he switched to gunny sacks. Usually when it was necessary to use gunny sacks, they were fastened to the mule by several thicknesses of belt webbing, but webbing had not been provided, either. The only binding available was in the form of pieces of hard leather about three inches wide. When these were cinched to the mules, they went wild and packs were strewn across the prairie. So Alfred switched to his wagons, each drawn by four mules. He was forced to throw away tents and everything but the barest supplies of food and ammunition.

His force was big enough and strong enough[4] to establish Fort Rice a week after he had started. There he left behind 300 men to build and man the post so that he could use it as a supply base.[5] As he traveled north, he left behind smaller detachments in less fortified positions so that he would have a supply line on his return.

The going was rough. The heat and drought had left a layer of dust over the plains that rose up to choke even the most hardy. Water was the greatest problem. What little water the column could find was full of alkali and not fit to drink. When they did find a water hole eight inches deep, Sully placed a guard around it with the men only ten paces apart; but the animals stampeded and stood in it during the night, so that it, too, was not fit to drink.

When he reached the Heart River, Sully knew that the Indians were less than a hundred miles away. He felt that he was within

En route to Yellowstone country, Sully's army included nearly 5,000 men, 15 Missouri River steamboats, and 300 wagon teams.

striking distance, so he dumped his emigrant train as well as his supplies. By this time the emigrants were used to the comfortable feeling of having thousands of troops around them. When they learned that Alfred intended to leave them behind, they were in turn irate, suppliant, disconsolate, and resigned to die. Alfred told them that a few hundred men would be more than enough to protect them and that he could ill afford to spare even this many for he knew not what was ahead. In panic they dug rifle pits and prepared to shoot their horses so they could hide behind the carcasses in the event of an Indian raid. Sully looked on in disgust and then left to find the Indians.

It was eighty miles to the Indian camps, and they were waiting for him. As he had predicted, they had banded together: Santee Sioux, Teton Sioux, Unkpapas, Blackfeet, Minneconjous, and Yanktons were all fighting together—an unprecedented force of between 5,000 and 6,000 warriors. Alfred's fighters at this point

185

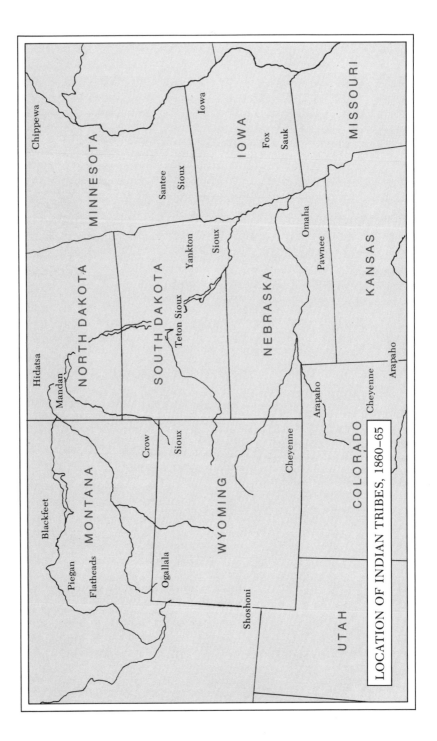

LOCATION OF INDIAN TRIBES, 1860–65

numbered about 2,000. Bragging was a common trait among the Indians; they were bold and arrogant, and asked him why he had come to die: "If he has no ears, we will give him ears; if he has ears, we will cut them off."

Their camp was at the base of a mountain called *Tah-kah-ha-kuty*, or Kildeer, and covered enough ground to house 110 bands of Sioux. The squaws, children, and old men gathered at the base of the mountain to watch the braves make good their boast that this battle meant the annihilation of the white man.

It was not the usual battle scene. No bugles sounded the charge; no Indian war cries filled the air; even the spectators remained silent and motionless. There was a deadly quiet around Kildeer. The soldiers dismounted and formed a line of skirmishers. Every fourth soldier stood just behind the line, holding his own horse and three others. A few bold braves rode out within firing distance to reconnoiter and survey the line of soldiers. Then they wheeled and rode back to join the lines of mounted warriors.

Slowly the two waves of men came toward each other, foot by foot. The faces on both sides reflected a calm, quiet confidence and determination. The only sound was the rumble of thousands of horses' hooves and the measured tread of the foot soldiers.

When the first shots were fired, everything changed. The Indians charged and filled the air with battle yells and war whoops. Their charge was repelled, and they wheeled to fall back, reload, and charge again. The soldiers moved forward in a steady, slow advance.

Alfred did not want a charge, nor did he want hand-to-hand combat. He was anxious to try out his artillery on the Indians. Darkness had prevented this at White Stone Hill. While the battle was going on at Kildeer, he quietly moved his cannon to the flanks, where it could command a sweeping view of the flat land in front of the mountain. This would give him enfilade fire, where he could sweep through an entire line of Indians from the side, rather than the less damaging frontal fire, where a shot might simply make a small hole in the line.

He waited until they fell back to reload within his line of fire, and then his cannon began their barrage. Eight guns killed a hundred and fifty Indians within a few minutes. That was all it took. Panic took hold of the Indians and the warriors, half naked, fled into the mountains. So confident had they been of victory that they had let the soldiers get within half a mile of their camp before they thought of striking their lodges. The squaws, children, and old men followed the warriors. The camp was left standing, and the soldiers marched in.

Sully sent four companies of the Eighth Minnesota to clear the Indians off the top of the mountain, and the troops watched them flee into the Bad Lands. While the loss of life, prestige, and confidence was a great blow to the Indians, the loss of their supplies was an even greater blow. They faced a winter in the Bad Lands without food, clothing, or shelter.

The soldiers slept that night in the Indian camp after burying their dead. The next day they burned the lodges and everything in them, and killed the dogs lest small parties return and find them useful. Alfred wanted to make sure that they would not survive to return again in force, and he planned to pursue them. But first he had to return to pick up his intolerably bothersome band of emigrants.

He had covered 172 miles in six days, including one day for the battle and time out to burn the Indians' possessions and to bury the dead. His men were trail-tired, and he was tempted to take them back to Fort Rice to rest before continuing the pursuit. Also, he was not anxious to take the emigrant train through the Bad Lands and probably hoped he could leave them at Fort Rice. But in checking his supplies he found that the commissary at the fort had erred in providing him with rations, and he had only enough for six days. He could not make the fort. He decided to go on and hunt down the Indians even though the odds were against him.

Sully's column, again accompanied by the emigrant wagons, set out in a torturous march from the Heart River to the Bad

Lands. The intense heat swelled the tongues of the weary soldiers and settlers so much that by ten in the morning no verbal order could be given—the men could not even speak, much less bark out a command. To counteract this as much as possible, Alfred set reveille at three o'clock, march by five; the average march was twenty miles a day, and the troops had to quit, exhausted and bone dry, by three in the afternoon.[6] Many animals collapsed along the way and had to be shot.

By August 5 the force had reached the eastern rim of the Bad Lands. Colonel Thomas reported that Sully took one look and termed it "truly hell with the fires burned out." The rim fell away to a basin six hundred feet below with an elaborate labyrinth of canyons walled in by high, almost insurmountable buttes. It was forty miles across, with no sign of vegetation or water. The canyons were so narrow in places that even a mule would have trouble getting through; for a wagon they were impossible. Sully's officers urged him not to try to get through; the emigrants were sure they would all die. But an Indian boy said he had been through a long time ago with his tribe and he thought he could find the way.

Alfred Sully was obsessed with the idea of destroying the Indians or weakening them to the extent that they would never again be able to strike in force. He had orders to cross the Yellowstone and it lay across the Bad Lands; there was no way to go but forward. He told the Indian boy to lead the way, leaving it up to the emigrant train, many of whom were seeking gold, to come with him or go off on their own. They elected to follow him.

Through miles of virtually impassable, tortuous trails they went, cutting roads for the emigrant wagons to get through narrow spaces. An estimated one thousand Indians appeared on the buttes above and watched in silence. When the buttes were low enough, the Indians harassed them with a rain of arrows. Where they could find footing, the braves climbed down to ledges and fired from there. The buttes were too steep to climb, but occasionally Alfred found a place wide enough for his cannon, and

189

he fired up the cliffs into the most likely spots for ambuscades.

All the while, Sully was sick. He suffered from rheumatism and dysentery, and unable to mount a horse, was forced to ride in a wagon. But still he urged his men on even though horses and men alike frequently tumbled over steep embankments when the trail led over the top of a butte.

The Indians attacked in force on August 7. From the top of a 500-foot butte, they rained arrows down on the column, which was penned in a gorge too narrow for wagons to maneuver. Pandemonium broke loose among the emigrants; horses reared and scraped against the rock walls. The artillery was ineffective, except to clean out an occasional ambush on the side of the cliff.

The Indians actually did not do much damage, nor did they want to come down and fight. Sully did not move as night was coming on to bring an end to the impasse. Having time to plan his next move, he called Colonel Thomas[7] to him and said, "Have everything ready to move at six o'clock in the morning, in perfect fighting order; put one of your most active field officers in charge of a strong advance guard, and you will meet them at the head of the ravine, and have the biggest Indian fight that will ever happen on this continent."[8]

The next morning, before six, Sully looked over the line of troops and told Thomas, "Those fellows can whip the devil and all his angels. Hold them well in hand, but push for the Indians' camp, if you can find it; they will fight for their families; protect your flanks and I will protect the rear. You must make history today."[9]

Sully seemed to have a sixth sense about what to expect of terrain. Surely enough, after Thomas led his mounted troops and batteries along a ravine barely wide enough for a wagon to pass through, the trail gradually climbed until his advance elements reported that they had reached a high plateau with a broad plain and that the Indians were gathered there in force. As the soldiers reached the crest the battle began. Indians surrounded Sully's men on three sides but the soldiers inched forward, while on the

190

slope leading to the top of the cliff the artillerymen pushed and tugged, sweated, strained, and cursed to get the cannon up to the flat land where it could go into action.

There was no question of frontal attacks with guidons flying and bugles blaring. It was flank and maneuver—hit your strongest blow, and then back away until you saw your next opening—and above all, take advantage of the terrain. Force them between the hills so you could hit them from the top of the crests. This was the way the Indians fought. They were masters of this strategy. But in this way the soldiers made way for the cannon to get up onto the field and into position. All was bedlam, with the Indians screaming, yelling, and firing. When the cannon opened fire, the noise was too much for the general. He mounted his horse and climbed to the plateau. Here he was helped down, and he sat on the ground, leaning back against a rock. Thomas reported to him, and Sully pointed to where he would find the Indian camp. The battle went back and forth for twelve miles before nightfall set in. They found the Indian camp where Alfred said it would be, but the Indians had gone.

The next day Sully went out on horseback looking for them but found only small bands; the battle lasted only an hour before the Indians broke up and fled in all directions. In the Battle of the Bad Lands, or, as it was known by the Indians, *Waps-chon-choka*, there were 8,000 warriors; of these 311 were killed and between 600 and 700 wounded. Sully lost only 9 killed and about 100 wounded.[10]

Here all necessity for future large expeditions against the Indians ceased. The Indians, broken up, scattered in all directions; forced to pass the winter without their lodges, without any winter supply of provisions, their horses gone, or in no condition to hunt, many of them starved to death; and had not the winter of 1864–1865 been remarkably mild, their suffering would have been very much greater; as it was, they were fully satisfied it was useless for them to contend against our Government. Very large numbers of them came to the different military posts on the frontiers during the winter, gave themselves up, swearing eternal friendship toward the whites, so by the summer of 1865 nearly all the Sioux in the Northwest were friends. The party who still held out were a portion of the Santees and the North Yanktonais, who had moved beyond the British line, under the protection of the British flag, where they could cross the frontier to commit depradations on our people, and retreat back over the frontier when pursued.

There was a tremendous difference between the Indians who gave themselves up and those who remained warlike. This is typified by the talks they gave when they came into the army posts for council meetings. Sully had a great respect for the Sioux. He thought they were in many ways superior to whites. They were proud, defiant, and unafraid. Here is a message delivered at one of their meetings with the Indian agent while Alfred was nearby:

To The Agent, greetings.

We have this day requested Mr. Pierre Gareau to deliver to you this our message:

It is our wish that you stop the boat belonging to Mr. Galpin at this place and send her back from here, as we do not want the whites to travel through our country. We claim both sides of the River and boats going above must necessarily pass through it.

We do not want the Whites to undertake to travel on our lands. The Traders we give permission to travel by Water but not by land, and boats carrying passengers we will not allow. If you pay no attention to what we are now saying to you, you may rely on seeing the tracks of my horses on the War Path.

And we for the last time beg of you to bring us no more presents, as we will not receive them; as yet we have never accepted your goods since you have been bringing them to us. A few of our people have been in the habit of receiving and re-

Following the disastrous winter of 1864–65, large numbers of Indians came to the military posts, swearing eternal friendship.

ceipting for them, but not with the consent of the Nations or the Chiefs, Soldiers and Head Men of our Camp.

We notified the "Bears Ribs" yearly not to receive your goods, but he had no ears and *we gave him ears by killing him.* We now say to you bring us no more; if any of our people receive any more from you, we will give them their Ears as we did to the Bear's Ribs.

We acknowledge no agent and we notify you for the last time to bring us no more Goods. We have told all the Agents the same thing but they have paid no attention to what we have said. If you have no Ears, we will give *you* Ears, and then your Father (The President) will not send us any more goods or Agents.

We also say to you, that we wish you to stop the whites from traveling through our country and if you do not stop them, we will. If your whites have not Ears, we will *give them Ears.*

193

The Whites in the country have been threatening us with soldiers; all we ask of you is to bring Men and not women dressed in Soldier Clothes. We do not ask for soldiers to fight without you refuse to comply with what we ask.

We have sent you several messages and we think you have never received them, otherwise we would of heard something from you; I am not even now certain that you will ever hear what I now say. You may get this, and then tear it up, and tell your Father that we are all quiet and receive your goods and by this means keep your place to fill your pockets with dollars, while our Great Father knows nothing of what is going on, but is like a Blind Old Woman, Can't See. We beg of you for once to tell our Great Father what we say and tell him the truth.

> Signed by the Chief Men of the Unkpapas
> Village (*viz*)

1. The Bald Eagle; 2. The Red Hail; 3. The One That Shoots Walking; 4. The Little Bear; 5. The Crow That Looks; 6. The Bear Heart; 7. The Little Knife; 8. The Feather Tied to His Hair; 9. White at Both Ends.

Alfred respected the Sioux, and while he welcomed them as adversaries, he regretted having to kill them. He had no respect for other tribes, like the Rees, Gros-Ventres, and Mandans, and would not even fight them. The talks they made at the council meetings were indicative of their stature in Sully's eyes.

This was the speech of White Chief, principal chief of the Rees:

I am glad to meet my white friends here and it makes my heart glad.

We have tried to keep the country open and free from hostile Indians and now you have come to help us.

Father, we are glad to see you again. Here in this place the hostile Indians rob us every day, and I hope you will kill some of them.

194

You are the General, the head man, and you have your officers and I would like to have some of my men help me and be
chiefs and I want to get dresses for them. What you say to your
officers is all one word, and I am the same here in my Medicine
Lodge I would not say anything that is not true.

We have three nations here, and we have three head chiefs,
and we want soldiers so that we can keep the law.

I listen to you and my great white father and I like your
council.

We like what you say that the traders must not sell whiskey,
and we hope you will not allow them to sell whiskey to the
Indians.

We used to get presents from the government every year, but
this year we have got nothing and we don't know the reason.

We used to go on the boats when they came and get a cup of
coffee but now they don't allow us to and we don't know why.

You have a church and this lodge is my church and I want
your men to respect it.

Crow Breast, principal chief of the Gros-Ventres, said:

We never do anything wrong and the Forts are all friendly
to us.

I remember what you told me last year and I tried to get the
Indians to come in here and trade but they would not come.

Since last year I have lost four hundred horses.

The hostile Indians that are around here are not the ones
that stole my horses, but the Indians from below that have
treaties with the Government, and the Yanktons and others.

Father you see we are poor, and I can't get enough to eat,
for when I go to hunt they drive me in.

Our traders used to give us a feast, but now they don't
look at us.

I think you will give me some good advice how to get my
horses back.

The Yanktons stole forty-two horses from me.

It is fourteen years since we came from Fort Laramie, and I have lost a great many men, but we always try to do as you say.

I am pleased to meet with you and hear you speak.

Alfred must have been more than slightly nauseated by this speech. He predicted that some Sioux tribes would fight on, but that many of the non-Sioux tribes, including those he had just heard, would die of sickness and starvation. The principal causes of death, Alfred thought, would be venereal disease and malnutrition resulting from false hopes of handouts.

S ULLY'S TROUBLES DID NOT END with the defeat of the Indians. For four days the troops, horses, and emigrants had been without water, save what they could scoop up out of occasional water holes. His entire force was on one-third rations and, although he knew the general direction in which the Yellowstone ran, he was not sure how far it was.

But there was nothing to do but go on. On the tenth of August he decided to risk the blazing sun and start late so as to give his men a chance to rest. In an area where there was not a blade of grass, his animals died of hunger if they did not die of thirst. "By noon of the 10th the route was lined for miles with dead horses and abandoned wagons. Ragged, thirsty, barely able to stagger, the column struggled on."[11]

That day one of Alfred's scouts brought him a wood chip. A small thing, but it meant salvation. Such a chip could have come only from the fuel burned by a riverboat. He passed the word to his entire command. Crippled force or no, the last ten miles were made at a full gallop, and all discipline was cast aside when they reached the river. Men drank of it, swam in it, rolled in it—clothes and all. Deer and elk were plentiful, and fresh meat

196

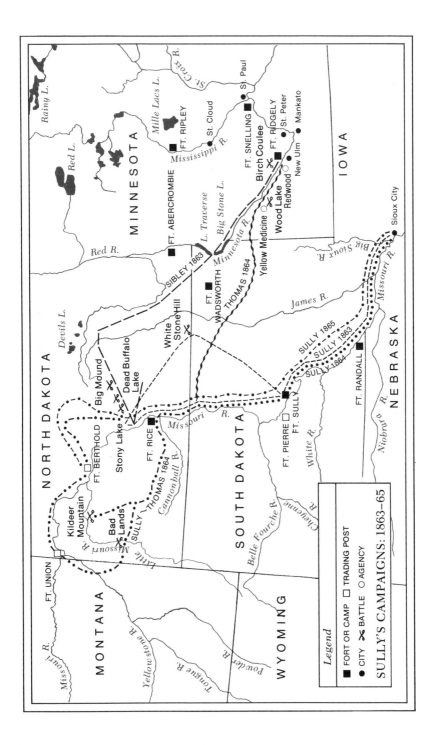

SULLY'S CAMPAIGNS: 1863–65

Legend

■ FORT OR CAMP □ TRADING POST
● CITY ✗ BATTLE ○ AGENCY

was the order of the day. And there were two boats, the *Alone* and the *Chippewa*, loaded with their supplies. A third boat, carrying the material with which Alfred was to build a fort on the Yellowstone, had sunk. It is not likely he mourned it, for this relieved him of an arduous and, in his opinion, unnecessary task.

Once again he was on his way home, and he had a special reason for wanting to get there. He was going to be married again. He crossed the Yellowstone. Nine emigrants drowned in the crossing, but it is hardly likely that Alfred gave this a second thought because of his inveterate dislike for the emigrants whom he regarded as nothing better than leeches. Better they than his soldiers. On the other side, he and the emigrants parted company; the wagon train, safe from Indians now, headed west while Sully headed east and south.

On his way back to Fort Ridgely he stopped at Fort Union. Here he found a situation that caused his temper to flare. Kenneth McKenzie of the American Fur Company had founded what was known as Fort Union in 1829 to compete against rival fur companies. By sharp tactics, he was able to best them all. His wile was to send men out to meet the Indians who were coming in with pelts, give them gifts, and then induce them into his stockade. Once they were in, the gates were closed and the liquor, from McKenzie's private still, flowed freely. When the Indians and their squaws awoke the next morning, they could not remember what they had traded for, and they had nothing to show for their months of trapping except a hangover.

Alfred was infuriated at McKenzie's practices, particularly since he had just come from fighting the Indians and he blamed most of the Indian troubles on the traders' illegal traffic in liquor. He placed troops at Fort Union, making it a military installation for the first time. The following year Fort Union went out of business as a trading post and its buildings were sold to the government.[12]

Alfred was relieved and happy to rid himself of the irritant emigrants who bothered him so much. They pushed on for gold in spite of his warning that the country was unsafe and vegetation sparse. His joy was short-lived. By the time he reached Fort Rice on September 8, he was advised that an emigrant train had been besieged by a band of almost three thousand Indians about three hundred miles west of the fort. He dispatched 850 men to bring them back to the Missouri. While they were glad to be rescued, most of them were furious that he would not escort them to the Yellowstone.

Chapter Eleven

The Indian Question

WHEN NEWS OF SULLY'S CAMPAIGNS became the subject for discussions in Washington, ugly rumors began to circulate about his brutal treatment of the Indians. He was accused of merciless annihilation of the enemy by using cannon against a defenseless people, although he had used his cannon only as an instrument of war in regularly-fought battles. On the way back from the campaigns, his volunteer soldiers had defiled and robbed the Indian catafalques along the way, but Sully did not hear of these depredations until complaints were filed. By this time, the volunteers, whose enlistments had expired, had already been discharged from the army. Charges of brutality were circulated by Indian agents he had dismissed from the service, particularly Dr. Walter Burleigh, who had gone to Washington for the expressed purpose of discrediting him.

Alfred could defend himself against these charges, but as they gained momentum Congress had to act. It appointed a committee to investigate "the condition of the Indian tribes and their treatment by the Civil and Military authorities of the United States." James R. Doolittle of Wisconsin was named chairman. When members of the committee came west, Sully was ordered to give them his full cooperation, even to the point of providing protection for them to visit the tribes and see for themselves.

Ordered to speak out, he welcomed the opportunity of explaining what he thought could and should be done for the Indians. So that he would not be misquoted, he asked the committee members to put their questions in writing, and he answered them in the same way. His contempt for the press was no secret. He held the reporters and publishers responsible for the ugly rumors about his activities, regarding them as scavengers who earned a living by publishing false stories that would create a sensation and thus magnify their importance.

> Headquarters, N.W.
> Indian Expedition
> Sioux City, Iowa
> June 10, 1865

Hon. J. R. Doolittle,

Chairman, Congressional Committee

Sir: Your communication of May 10th I received a few days ago, and in replying to it I will answer your questions as they are numbered in your letter:

1st—Since I first entered the Army in 1841, with the exception of the time during the Mexican War, and the first two years of the Rebellion (when I was South), I have been, I may say, constantly in the Indian Country. I have been with the Seminoles of Florida, with the various tribes of Indians in Southern California, Oregon, and the eastern part of California, with all the bands of the western or Teton Sioux, with the Omahas, Poncas, Pawnees, Cheyennes, Rees, Mandans, Gros-Ventres and Crows.

2nd—The tribes that came in close contact with the Whites and civilization are fast decreasing. Changes in their mode of life, and in the fact of their learning all the vices and few of the virtues of the whites is in my opinion the cause of their decreasing.

3rd—Venereal diseases, among those who have been living near settlements also whiskey are the diseases most common. Small pox often is introduced among different tribes by accident and is very fatal.

4th—Intoxication prevails to some extent among tribes that live near settlements, but as a general rule, with the exception of the very old men and old squaws, I do not think the Indians can be considered addicted to intoxication. Among some of the wild tribes, I have known them utterly to refuse to have anything to do with it. This I am told by traders who have tried to sell it to them. But the Indian, like the White man, if he lives where whiskey is plenty, will acquire a taste for it, and when he does will become as debased as the lowest white drunkard. It is already against the law to introduce Whiskey into the Indian Territory, but it is evaded. Large quantities are brought from the British line, by English Half Breeds, to trade, and this is impossible for us to prevent, without our troops can get permission to cross the frontier. I think we have laws enough on the subject, if they were only enforced.

5th—There is a very wide and remarkable difference in different tribes in regard to prostitution; while some tribes are disgustingly loose in their habits, there are other tribes, living in the same country, who are remarkable for their virtue. The Rees Indian, for example carry this vice to a great extent and disease in a fearful state is fast destroying the nation. On the contrary the females of most of the wild bands of Sioux on the plains called the Teton Sioux, set an example of virtue worthy of being copied by any white civilized nation. I believe the contact with depraved specimens of white population, a taste for luxuries, only to be procured by money, are the principal causes of the females falling into this vice. When they do, they become very much depraved and disease naturally follows.

6th—I know of no other facts that are the cause of their decay; a total change of the system now adopted towards the

Indians will in the end effect a remedy. I have given much of my attention to this subject and feel sure that with a proper system in our Indian Affairs, the Indians who are now a curse and a nuisance to the country can be made a peaceful part of our community if not a beneficial part.

7th—As regards the system of making Reservations, and pushing the Indians from the East, from the West, from the North and from the South, and concentrating them into one section of the country, it has been, in my opinion, a very bad policy. At a great expense the Government has been taking trouble away from one section of the country, and concentrating it on the borders of another. I do not altogether disapprove of the system of Indian Reservations, but I do of the constant changes of Reservations.

8th—It is best that the lands should be held in severalty. . . . I would not propose to confer the power of alienation of real estate upon Indians for this generation at least, but their children who after they have been civilized and educated, should have the right, when they have arrived at the proper age, to do what they please with their property.

9th—There is a very great difference in regard to the amount of agriculture the different tribes of Indians attend to. Among these nomadic tribes who live in a country abounding with game, with wild fruits and roots, that can be eaten, it is hard to bring them down to cultivate the soil. Their instinct teaches them to wander out on the prairie to hunt, and the section of the country they inhabit is ill fitted for agricultural purposes. In the children of such tribes I would inculcate a taste to raise stock, like the Jesuit priests did in their missions in California. All who have lived in California before it was settled, can testify to their success and the immense herds of cattle belonging to these Indian Missions. With other tribes, such as the Rees, Mandans, Gros-Ventres, and several tribes in Arizona whose names I cannot recollect, cultivation of the soil is carried on with great success. . . . Most of the work however, is done by the squaws. The he-Indian is too proud to work. His duties are war and the chase. As regards half-breeds, I regard theirs a very bad mixture. As a general rule they retain too many of the bad qualities of the Indians and too few of the good qualities of the Whites.

10th—Schools and education have not been attended as much as they should be. Congress appropriates money for this purpose, but little of it, generally, is expended in schools. I recommend that the children, male and female, of the Indians be made to go to school, that the boys be taught to work at different trades, the girls to sew, wash and cook, and above all teach them the habits of cleanliness. Do this, and you do all required to reclaim the savage, and make him a useful human being.

11th—In regard to the country called Indian Territory ... the Indians should hold their lands, but they should as far as possible be separated to destroy as far as possible the feeling they have of being a separate nation, of which they are proud. By degrees as they become educated and civilized, they will consider themselves citizens of the United States and be proud of that.

12th—Money annuities should be *entirely* discontinued. It is the principal source of all our trouble at Indian Agencies. . . . It is my *opinion* that very little of it reaches the hands of the Indians. . . . As a general thing the greater part of the annuities is already pledged to the trader at the agency for goods furnished before it is paid, and the Indians rarely see any of the money. . . . I don't think much of the Indian annuities are squandered for intoxicating drink for the simple reason that *the* trader, for there is only one allowed, pockets most of the money. . . . Don't make any money payments to the Indians. Issue them clothing and supplies when they are in need of them.

13th—The operation of the order system is very bad. Very frequently I have seen, during an annual Indian payment, nearly all the Indians of the nation collected waiting weeks and months for the goods to arrive, and every day being told that their supplies will reach soon. They would wait more patiently than any body of white men would, till their small stock of provisions they had on hand would become exhausted and their families almost starving. Then the Agent would give the Indians orders on the trader at the place, by which the trader pockets all the money due the Indian, half starved, not knowing what he pays or the value of what he buys. As a general rule, but one trader is allowed at an agency. His prices he and the agent regulate. At least the goods are near at hand and the payment must take place. The agent then persuades a number of his Indians to go on a hunt, and while this number is away, the goods are distributed to those who remain.

14th—The Indian Department unquestionably should be under the War Department. It is to the troops the friendly Indian looks for protection against hostile bands, and from the troops the Agent or Trader looks for protection when his Indians, exasperated at repeated impositions, threaten to take his life. The Secretary of the Interior may believe our policy best to adopt towards certain bands, and the Secretary of War may think it necessary to act quite differently. Thus different orders are issued to the Agents and troops; frequently, Indians become so troublesome, it is necessary to turn them over to the hands of the military, and in the midst of the War, before peace and quiet is established, the agent or some other official is empowered to make a treaty and pay the Indians large sums to behave themselves. It is a common saying among the Indians that when they are in want of more annuities, all they have to do is kill a few white men and steal a few horses.

15th—In setting apart Reservations it should be done by the Department, we acting and justly towards the Indians. It could be done by treaty, but it amounts to the same thing, for the Indians can neither read nor write nor understand our language, and is at our mercy. The service of an interpreter has to be used, frequently some unprincipalled half-breed whom speculators can bribe to interpret just what they like. What is to prevent these Indians from signing the purport of which they know nothing about. Many of our Indian treaties are made in this way and then we say the Indian refuses to live up to his treaty.

16th—I approve very much of the placing of orphan children in the families of Christians for education and civilization.

17th—In order to better the condition of the Indians, and protect him from frauds, I would have the Indian Agencies stationed at Military Posts, the Commanding Officer being the Superintendent. At each post there should be an agent; there should also be established missionary schools. The annuity goods should be purchased by someone directed for that purpose and sent to the Post. On its arrival, the Commanding Officer should order a council of the three senior officers to examine the goods, compare them with the invoices and with the price current, of the city where these goods are purchased, and then to hand in their report, under oath, that the amount expended for the goods is correct, to the Commanding Officer, to be forwarded by him. The goods should be distributed in the presence of officers and under the orders of the Commanding Officer. If this plan is adopted, I doubt if you would find as many persons in the country seeking the position of Indian Agents, for then there would be no chance of their making a fortune on a salary of $1500 a year.

To show what good can be done in the way of improving the Indian race and making them useful, I would call your attention to the various missions in New Mexico and California. If you travel over that country you will be surprised at the magnificent buildings you will occasionally meet with in the midst of a desert or deserted country. They are called missions of some saint or other. These buildings and all the improvements, flourishing fields, mills, herds of cattle, etc., is the work of a few priests and the wild Indians. Now I am not a Catholic, nor do I wish to advocate any particular sect or religion, but this I must say are actuated by a desire to promote the interest of his church. You may call it fanaticism if you will, but it is sincere and there is no selfish personal feeling in it. The wild savage soon sees this and appreciates it. Then again, their forms of religious ceremony; there is a mystery, a solemnity, that strikes the ignorant Indian with awe, or as they term it "Big Medicine". We all know that the Catholic Church, like dress parades and grand reviews in the armies, that affect the discipline of the Church or Army.

I therefore think that the mission I recommended above be placed in the hands of the Catholic Clergy in preference to any other sect. Another thing I would recommend at these military and religious stations in the Indian Country, and that is the organizing by degrees of a military force of Indians. I would begin with a few at first. I would use this force as a police force in the village, and as pickets and scouts. By degrees I would increase the force and enforce discipline more strictly, and if the hostile bands attacked my Indians, I would make an Indian War on them by offering a reward for the scalp of any warlike Indians. I would send parties and capture the women and children. Make the women work at the mission, and the children, by force. This may sound unchristianlike, but with the savages a woman is treated as bad as any negro slave formerly was in our country, and it would be a mercy to her to be under the control of a Christian Mission.

After the War was over, allow the husband and father to visit their squaws and children and if, after they had been in charge of the mission as prisoners, if they wished to rejoin their husbands, or the husbands to come and live at the missions, let them do so. By locating these missions under the protection of troops, in a few years they would be flourishing settlements, strong enough to protect themselves, and as soon as they became sufficiently strong and civilized, withdraw the troops, and let them have all the benefits of the laws of the country, like any white man. They certainly have an equal right to the land we occupy, and as soon as they are fitted for it they have the right to be citizens of the United States, and in every respect made amenable to our laws. When they transgress them they should be punished, and if the civil authorities are not able to enforce the laws, then the Military should be called on. I believe in separating the bands of Indians as widely apart as possible, thus destroying their individuality, their nationality. So far from concentrating them and treating them as we do a foreign nation, it would be better, when people wished the land belonging to the Indians instead of pushing them into wilderness, to purchase a tract of land, even in some of our densely populated eastern states, and place them there. In a few years, they would be forced to adopt the habits of civilized life, or they would soon become extinct.

I will take an example of this case, the Minnesota Sioux. Not many years ago the different bands of this nation were established on the Mississippi. Wabash's band at the town of Wabasha, Red Wing's band at Red Wing. When it became necessary to settle that country, and send them on their Reservations up the St. Peter or Minnesota River, it would have been far better to say to them: We must have your land. Each family will select his locality or farm. Settlers would then be allowed to settle around each separate band. Of course in consideration of the land taken from them the Government would assist them in cattle, agricultural implements and establishing schools for the instruction of their children and let them know they were protected in law in all their rights, the same as the white man. In regard to reservations now in existence I would adopt the same rule. There are only two rules to follow: one is to drive them off further, starve them and drive them to desperation, till we have to adopt some other mode of ridding ourselves of an encumbrance. The other rule is to reclaim them from their savage life, and by kindness and education make them peaceable, if you cannot make them useful members of our community, but don't send Indian Agents and traders among them to rob them of what the Government appropriates for their improvement.

Alfred's letter to the committee reflected nearly a lifetime of dealing with the Indians. More than a decade after he left California, it was to the mission system that he turned to find an appropriate model for civilizing the Indians. Through the bitterness of his early army career, the years of sadness that followed his beloved Manuela's death, and the bloody experiences of both fratracidal war and extermination campaigns, his appreciation for the humanity and character of his red adversaries remained intact.

Chapter Twelve

Out to Pasture

WHEN ALFRED SULLY RETURNED from the Yellowstone, he had hoped to marry Sophia Webster, the "mystery lady" of his Richmond experience, and settle down at the post for at least a little while. But General Grant had other plans for him. Regardless of what most people thought of General Pope, Grant, who was then commander of the armies of the United States, regarded him as an able administrator. On November 30, 1864, he called Pope to the headquarters of the Army of the Potomac in Virginia and told him that he had created a new geographical command, the Division of the Missouri, to bring together the departments of the Northwest, Missouri, and Kansas under a single head. Pope was to be the commanding officer of this new jurisdiction, with Sully as one of the principal subordinates. With the end of the Civil War in sight, Grant wanted the Indian situation resolved once and for all.

Pope must have been flattered by the new command. He wasted no time planning his campaign to subjugate the Sioux. But the bad luck that had dogged his impulsive actions at Bull Run and the lack of judgment he had displayed during Sully's earlier campaigns against these Indians were still evident even as he mapped his strategy. His tactics called for three thrusts: the first, with 1,200 men under General Ford, would move against the tribes south of Arkansas; the second, with 1,200 men under General Sully, would push across Dakota north of the Black Hills and establish the Powder River fort, so that supplies which were already stockpiled at Fort Union could be shipped there; and the third, with 2,000 men, under General Connor, would march against the Powder River Indian camps and join forces with Sully.[1]

The campaign was supposed to start in May but ran into the usual delays. Supplies were slow in coming; units were not up to strength; enlistments were expiring; and finally, with the end of the Civil War, Pope was deluged with reassigned troops who arrived without mounts. They were furious at the thought of being sent to fight Indians and deserted by the hundreds.

To add to Pope's woes, members of the Doolittle committee came poking about, disrupting routine duty and demanding protection to visit the Indian tribes in his territory. Even to this day, the arrival of an investigating committee at a military installation causes uneasiness and uncertainty on the part of both officers and enlisted men, and the expenditure of a considerable amount of time and effort on spit-and-polish at the expense of the job at hand. When the investigating committee is a congressional committee headed by a senator, the troops walk as if they were treading on eggs. There is little doubt that this group disturbed Pope's preparations, particularly since this visit was the spearhead for a peace offensive being mounted by Congress in opposition to Pope's policy of aggression in preference to bribing the Indians with annuities. He stated: "The treaties I have directed military commanders to make are simply an explicit understanding with the Indians that so long as *they* keep the peace the United States will keep it, but as soon as they commit hostilities the military forces will attack them, march through their country, establish military posts in it, and, as a natural consequence, their game will be driven off or killed."

In quoting this statement in *Frontiersmen in Blue*, Robert M.

211

Utley observes, "Such a treaty would cost nothing and, he believed, prove far more effective in maintaining the peace. Far from aiding any commission bent upon concluding the usual form of treaty he would employ his military forces to prevent it unless otherwise instructed by superior authority."[2]

Pope was exceeding his authority in trying to substitute his own policies for those of the Congress, and "as the summer wore on, the resolution with which the War Department supported the aggressive designs of the generals on the Plains weakened and finally collapsed."[3] Sully was ordered to give full support and protection to the committee.

Meanwhile Pope's plans were completely changed as a result of the actions of the Indians. During the previous winter British traders had visited the Indians, selling arms and ammunition, and inciting the Santee, Teton, and Yankton Sioux to unite and take up the fight in the spring of 1865. When they began to raid in Dakota and Minnesota, Pope did not foresee a full-scale war and panic, but he had to yield to the demands for action. He relieved Sully of his intended mission and assigned him to take an expedition into that territory. Sully was to make peace with them if possible, or fight them if necessary.

Sully sent out word to the Indians that he would talk peace with them at Fort Rice. He could not have picked a more unlikely place. Rice was under the command of a twenty-three-year-old parade ground officer, Col. Charles A. R. Dimon. On April 12 he had executed two Santee prisoners in reprisal for a raid in which they had not participated—they were in his jail at the time of the raid. Dimon's soldiers had the reputation of shooting first and then finding out whether the Indian they had killed was friend or foe; and if any band of Indians neared the fort there were full-scale attacks by the soldiers. Understandably, the Indians shunned Fort Rice.[4]

When Sully arrived at Rice by boat, the overeager Dimon fired an artillery salute to the commanding general of the district, and 130 lodges of Indians on their way to the parley thought they were going to be massacred, and fled. When boats carrying supplies arrived, those Indians already at the fort concluded that this meant that more soldiers were on the way, and they too fled. As a result, instead of the 3,000 lodges Sully expected to show up, there were only 200.

He vented his wrath on Colonel Dimon, reporting to Pope that Dimon was causing nothing but trouble and that he was too young and too rash for his position. He sent Dimon to Washington on an "important mission" and put the veteran Lieutenant Colonel Pattee of the Seventh Iowa Cavalry in command of Fort Rice. It was fortunate that he did. Sitting Bull had no faith in the peace talks, and as soon as he saw Sully head north, he attacked Fort Rice with five hundred warriors. Pattee was a rough-and-tumble, buckskin-and-moccasin soldier; although he was greatly out-numbered, he defeated the Sioux in a three-hour battle, thanks to his experience and his professional handling of his howitzers.

Sully had sent out word that he would meet the Indians at Fort Berthold, farther up the Missouri. But when word of Sitting Bull's raid on Fort Rice reached them, the Indians felt that Sully would be angry, and that instead of talking peace, he would set a trap to punish them. So again they stayed away.

While Sully's mission failed, so did those of Connor and Ford. The three groups with 5,000 men killed 100 Indians during the course of the summer—less than the number killed by troops protecting emigrant trains and settlements.[5] This did nothing to cool Sully's wrath. He went contrary to army policy and contrary to his own humane principles against scalping and mutilating when he said that it was no longer practical to send large bodies of troops after small bands of Indians who could elude them. He suggested that a bounty on scalps would be cheaper and more effective. While the government did not give the white man carte blanche to kill Indians and get paid for it, no forces such as those that had been fighting at Kildeer and in the Bad Lands were ever sent into the field against the Indians again. Even Custer's famous "army" numbered only 264 soldiers.

213

When Sully returned from his expedition of 1865, his combat days were over. But he continued to fight. He fought the army system, and he fought the government's policy of dealing with the Indians. And as a man who had lived a life of hardship beyond normal human endurance, he waged a battle for his life—he was critically sick.

His greatest wish was to have his temporary rank of brevet general made a permanent army rank, and he pulled all the strings at his command. On February 15, 1866, Gen. William T. Sherman, with whom he had served in California and upon whom he had counted as a friend, wrote:

> I doubt if any general officers will be retained in the new army. We advised 5 major and 10 brigadier generals in excess of the present number. I think the Army will be made of 12 cavalry and 50 infantry regiments, which will make a good many colonels and field officers.
>
> Look out for your own interests. I will have little to say and must in honesty favor those officers who clung to my fortunes from Shiloh to Raleigh. I assure you I wish you well, but caution you that all of the generals of volunteers will soon be mustered out.[6]

On April 10, 1866, Alfred and thirty-one other generals were mustered out of the regular army, their service "no longer being required."[7] All officers belonging to his personal staff were transferred or discharged. He retained his permanent army rank and was permitted to be called general, but as far as he was concerned, his career was finished.

He took an eight-month leave of absence and got married to Sophia Henrietta Webster.

It must have been an unusual marriage. Alfred rarely mentioned Sophia in his infrequent letters home, although he did make reference to his two children, Albert Walter and Blanche. He never wrote of where he and Sophia had met or under what circumstances; all the information he gave was that she was a Southern sympathizer and that she had lived in Richmond.

After his marriage, Alfred's frequent letters to his sister Blanche either stopped—or are no longer extant. His need to talk with someone on paper was apparently transferred from Blanche to Sophia, and while his letters expressed little affection, the need to write them seemed to increase the older he got. He had never expressed love after the death of Manuela—he seemed to have hardened himself against being hurt again—yet the emotional ties existed, with both family and with Sophia. Had they not, he wouldn't have written at all.

When Alfred Sully reported back for duty on December 28, 1866, the army did not know what to do with him. He was far too young for retirement in his grade—he was forty-seven— outwardly too healthy for a medical discharge, and too experienced and too bitter for a younger officer who ranked him to want Sully around to peer over his shoulder and tell him what to do.

So the army did to Alfred exactly what it would do to an officer in his position today. It created jobs for him, jobs with high sounding titles but with no real responsibility—preferably jobs in out-of-the-way places. That tore away at his pride just as if they had gradually stripped him of all rank, insignia by insignia. The other officers knew it; the enlisted men knew it. But civilians did not know it, so it left him with some semblance of dignity and prestige.

Alfred knew what was happening to him: he was being let out to pasture, was expected to give up or drink himself to death. Most of the men in his position did—and a great portion of them do today.

But Alfred Sully didn't feel he was through, in spite of the indignities he suffered. First, he was put on a board for examination of candidates for promotion in the army—the same board that had passed him over for promotion in the army—but his violent objections caused this onerous and subservient assignment to last only six weeks before he was transferred.

He longed to get back into the field against the Sioux. But the Sioux were peaceful, so he took an assignment that would at least bring him back among them along the Upper Missouri. The Interior Department let him have this assignment from February to September of 1867. As much as he missed his family, he was back in his element—visiting the Sioux, sleeping in a tent, and cementing the peaceful relations that existed. His only responsibility, however, was writing reports back to Washington—he had demonstrated that he was a careful observer and a good writer—so the department could be safe in the knowledge that for the present, at least, relations with the Sioux were under control. For Sully it was a vacation.

In September he was called back to New York. After six months there as a member of the Retiring Board, he was able to go back west with an assignment for almost a year in command of a regiment and the District of the Upper Missouri out of Fort Harker, Kansas. He got back in the field only occasionally—the skirmishes with the Indians were few—but at least he was a fighting general again. He knew it would be short-lived. Washington could not have him bringing in any great victories. If he did, pressure might be brought to bear on the appropriate military and civilian authorities to listen to his plea to make his brevet rank a permanent one, and the promotion boards had already passed him over in favor of younger, less experienced men. Alfred made many enemies among his superiors because he was so outspoken and critical; but he also had some influential supporters in high places. So it was likely that the military wanted the glory to go to younger men they wanted to promote.

Before he left the Upper Arkansas in May 1869, Sully's famous lack of diplomatic skill got him into trouble with his commanding officer. He took on as an adversary Gen. George Armstrong Custer, a close personal friend of Gen. Phil Sheridan.

In July 1867, Custer had been convicted of deserting his command and going almost a hundred miles away to visit his wife. This, along with six other convictions, resulted in his suspension from rank and command, and forfeiture of pay for one year. He was spending his time hunting and fishing in Lake Erie when he received a letter from General Sheridan. It was from Fort Hays, Kansas, dated September 24, 1868, and was sent as a personal letter, not as one that would go through the proper channels. Sheridan told him, "Generals Sherman, Sully and myself, nearly all of the officers of your regiment, have asked for you, and I hope the application will be successful."[8]

In keeping with his typical brashness and his practice of either ignoring orders or acting without them when it suited his personal ambitions, Custer noted in his personal narrative that "knowing the application of Generals Sherman and Sheridan and the other officers referred to would meet with a favorable reply from the authorities at Washington, I at once telegraphed to General Sheridan that I would join him by the next train, not intending to wait the official order which I knew would be issued by the War Department."[9]

Sully had no love for Custer. Certainly he must have been wary of a man who made the jump from captain to brigadier general in one leap and proved to be as arrogant and undependable as Custer was. When Custer arrived at Fort Hays, Sully was out in pursuit of hostile Indians from Fort Dodge into northwestern Oklahoma. He no sooner returned than the animosity that existed between the two men became evident. Custer derided his efforts against the Indians. Sully and Custer had equal commands—a regiment—yet Alfred asked Sheridan to relieve Custer of his command because he was too arrogant, too impulsive, too undisciplined, and knew nothing about fighting Indians. Custer for his part scoffed at a fighting general who rode around in an ambulance (Sully was too sick to get on a horse).

Sheridan reprimanded Sully, telling him that "Custer should be allowed to regulate the affairs of his own regiment and should not be restrained from doing so," and sent Sully off on a mission to establish Camp Supply. As soon as Sully came back to his post in March 1869, Sheridan told him he was not satisfied with his

217

performance and had him placed on the unassigned list. General Sherman, who was probably the most powerful figure in the army at that point, reflected Sheridan's displeasure.

This may have been a contributing factor in the many transfers of station Sully was to endure, the many requests for leave he was to submit for the next eight years, almost to the time of his death. Seven weeks after he was placed on the unassigned list, waiting for orders that would take him he knew not where, he was sent to Montana as superintendent of Indians there. By September 23, 1870, he was starting another nerve-wracking seven-week wait for orders. He was assigned to the Nineteenth Infantry on December 15, then placed in command at Baton Rouge, Louisiana, from January 12 to July 9, 1871. His next assignment was in command again at Baton Rouge, and he was allowed only five days to report. He endured this for only two and a half months more before he had had enough. His only respite had been a leave to visit his father, who was critically ill in Philadelphia (Thomas Sully died on November 5, 1872).

Every move Alfred was forced to make was a step down the ladder. Bit by bit the general's achievements were being forgotten, and bit by bit the general was dying. Understandably, he became more and more bitter. He had to get away.

The army granted him sick leave from June 15 to December 11, 1873, after he submitted a surgeon's certificate showing that he was not fit for duty. He wrote to the adjutant general: "I am so very debilitated by long continued sickness that I do not believe I will be fit for any duty for some time and I am still troubled with the same sickness." The "same sickness" was diagnosed by the surgeon general's office as "prolapsus produced by excessive exertion." This diagnosis was made in February 1863, and the illness grew progressively worse; when he died, an autopsy revealed that he had suffered internal bleeding for forty-four months. His physical torture must have matched his mental anguish.

In February 1874, while Alfred was en route to take command

Alfred did this painting of his quarters at Fort Vancouver. His wife and his son are shown by the house that is now a museum.

of Fort Vancouver, Washington, he became so ill in Omaha that he could not report at what was to be his final assigned station until May 13. He was destined to remain at Fort Vancouver with his wife and two children until he died, but there would be two temporary assignments for him. One was a grubby little chore —investigation of the Fetterman Massacre; the other was participation in the Nez Perce Indian War. After this the forgotten general would be allowed to die in peace.

WILLIAM J. FETTERMAN was a brevet lieutenant-colonel stationed at Fort Phil Kearny. He was a glory seeker who vowed that with a handful of men he could whip all of the Indians on the plains and bring the wars to an end forever. Unfortunately, he was given his tragic chance.

Four days before Christmas in 1866 the fort had sent out a wood-cutting party to provide timber to finish the building of the fort—barracks, mess hall, administration buildings, and other necessary adjuncts to an army post, including the yet unfinished stockade. There was sporadic firing in the area in which the woodcutters were working and Fetterman, as the second in command, requested that he be allowed to take a detail to overcome the attackers or at least to protect the cutters' position. Col. H. B. Carrington, in command, gave Fetterman permission but at least twice admonished him that he was to protect the working party and that under no conditions was he to pursue the Indians.

Fetterman was thirsting for blood, as was Capt. Fred H. Brown, who had vowed to get the scalp of the Indian's leader, Red Cloud. When they had chased the Indians away, Fetterman, in direct violation of orders, pursued them. Within two hours, Fetterman, Brown, and sixty-five men were killed, scalped, stripped of their clothing, and mutilated beyond recognition.

Alfred's job was to find out who was liable. His commission started in Omaha and worked its way north, questioning everyone who might have some knowledge of the events. Witnesses were hard to find. In the end, strangely enough, the commission placed the blame, not on any of the participants, but on Gen. Philip St. George Cooke, charging that he had not placed adequate personnel at this particular post when less vulnerable posts were provided with parade ground soldiers. Carrington was removed from Fort Phil Kearny. As soon as the report of the commission was in, General Sherman removed Cooke from command as well.

So Alfred did the army's dirty work and was then slated to go back to Fort Vancouver to paint pretty pictures. But he had one champion left to keep him from going the way of all unwanted generals. Gen. Oliver O. Howard was a fighting man's general. He had been through Manassas, Bull Run, Fairfax Station, Fair Oaks, and the whole Peninsula Campaign with Alfred. He lost an arm at Fair Oaks, but in lieu of the normal two-month leave due him for this injury, he was out in two days recruiting for the army. Howard could not stomach weakness or a waste of good manpower. He could sense what was wrong with Alfred and wanted to salvage the man's sense of dignity and make him feel that he was still useful. He was one of the few men in positions of high command who remembered what Sully had done. Howard was in command of the Department of the Columbia, which included Fort Vancouver, so he took Alfred away from his permanent post and put him on detached duty during the Nez Perce expedition. Alfred served with Howard in Idaho from June 21 to September 23, 1877.

The Nez Perce War came about as a result of the same factors that had caused other Indian wars: the whites settled on their lands without treaties; they abrogated those treaties that were made; Indian agents held up annuity payments or simply put the money in their own pockets; the white men were selling whiskey to the Indians; and the Indians were being pushed back onto smaller and smaller pieces of less desirable ground.

The first significant treaty was made with the Nez Perce in 1855. At that time the Indians were clearly divided into separate bands: Wallawalla, Cayuse, Umatilla, Palouse, Coeur d'Alene, Spokan and other Nez Perce. Among these there was a treaty faction and a nontreaty faction. The whites selected one chief, Lawyer, to represent the group even though he had no authorization to speak for all of the separate bands. He was outspoken and friendly to the white cause. His was the treaty faction; they adopted the white man's ways and soon became powerless, with no strong head men and no warrior chiefs. Chief Joseph, father of the more famous chief who took his name when the old man died, signed the treaty on behalf of his tribe only because it guaranteed the boundaries of his land, an area almost three times the size of Rhode Island. When annuities finally began to arrive, six years after the treaty was signed, the old chief refused to accept the bribes, saying he had not given away anything.

The whites did not wait for the formality of the payment. By 1862 approximately 18,500 of them were living on Nez Perce land, and they had shipped almost three million dollars in gold from Nez Perce mines. So under a new treaty they bought still more land from Lawyer and his followers—almost six million acres at about eight cents per acre. Again it was to be paid for in annuities. Old Joseph still would not sign away his territory. On his death bed in 1871 he admonished his son, Hin-mah-too-yah-lat-kekht: "Never forget my dying words. This country holds your father's body. Never sell the bones of your father and mother."[10] Joseph took his father's name and assumed leadership of the tribe. He was not at all the menacing savage the white man associated with the name Indian. "There was something 'civilized' about him. He spoke intelligently and with moderation; he argued but was patient and kind; he seemed to believe that the days of the Indian wars against the whites were over and that the two races must somehow find ways to settle their problems peacefully."[11]

He maintained this position until May 1877, when General Howard, who had at first been lenient with the Nez Perce, was forced by Sherman to adopt a get-tough policy. Joseph had stead-fastly refused to give up any of his lands, but Howard realized that he could not force the whites who were already on the land to evacuate. So he gave Joseph thirty days to move his band, which, combined with the Indians who had joined him, totaled about six hundred people. Joseph realized that the cause was hopeless and began to move his troops north to the Clearwater River. Just two days after the expiration date in Howard's ultimatum, a small puni-tive force caught up with Joseph's band. The Indians sent out spokesmen to meet them under protection of a white flag. But the troops fired on them and "The Battle of White Bird Canyon" en-sued, signaling the start of the Nez Perce War, on June 17, 1877.

There followed an epic saga in the history of Indian warfare. Joseph's band of 350 warriors, diminished in number after each battle, outmaneuvered and outflanked more than 2,000 soldiers. The Indians forced their pursuers to chase them more than 1,300 miles in seventy-five days; they themselves covered more than 1,800 miles because they would double back over their own tracks to delay the troops. Fighting only defensive battles, the Indians would thrust, parry, and withdraw, getting away when it seemed utterly impossible for them to escape.

Howard personally led the frustrating pursuit. Contrary to popular belief, Joseph did not lead the Nez Perce. While he was their leader in peace, he realized that he was inexperienced in warfare, so the strategy was laid out each night by a council of chiefs under Chief Looking Glass. Joseph participated in these councils and assumed responsibility for protecting the women and children as well as the herds, which included about two thousand horses.[12]

The chase would lead Howard beyond the limits of his jurisdiction, through canyons and forests, over mountains and across gorges; there was sometimes a drop of as much as two hundred feet, and the wagons had to be let down perpendicular walls by rope, hand over hand.[13]

On June 17 the Indians started south to Horseshoe Bend, where they crossed the Salmon River; then they headed west, then northwest, crossing the Salmon again at Billy Craig Crossing, then east, where on July 4 they met troops under Capt. Stephen C. Whipple. They came out to talk, but Whipple's men violated the flag of truce and the fighting began. Whipple had Joseph's band cornered there at Cottonwood Creek, but the Indians outmaneuvered him and got away. Meanwhile Howard was only a few days behind his quarry. He crossed the Salmon, but when he tried to recross it at Billy Craig Crossing, the river had risen so high and the current had become so strong that he had to retrace his steps all the way to White Bird Creek to get his boats. He lost about six days.

By the time Sully arrived at Howard's base headquarters in Lewiston, the pursuit had already begun. He wrote in successive letters to Sophia:

> I can give you no news as I have not yet had a conversation with Howard. Everything is in an uncertain state. The troubles are serious enough, but not so bad as the newspapers report.

All are in a state of anxiety fearing more Indians may break out. Settlers are therefor leaving their farms and coming in to this town. . . .

Howard has left with the troops to Mt. Idaho and left orders for me to march out and take command. He then intends to return. This is just what I expected of him. I shall not go as I am unable to. I regret very much I came up here at all. . . .

I got a letter from Howard this morning early in answer to the letter I wrote. He tells me to remain here until he returns. He feels sure he knows where the Indians are fortified and will go for them as soon as the troops that came up with me reach him. In that case he will have a fight before the end of this week, but I do not believe the Indians are as near him as he thinks. There may be a party there who will fall back to lead the troops in the wrong direction. . . .

The people are very much down on Howard and blame him very unjustly. He writes me he did not expect me to go into any rough work but only to travel as far as a wagon could go. As soon as he returns here he wants to consult with me. Col. Watkins, the gentleman who was with Howard on Decoration Day, is here and told me he advised Howard to turn the whole business over to me, as I have had much experience in such matters. So you see my stay here is very indefinite, and I can tell nothing until I see him. Some of the officers of the 4th Artillery who came up on the boat with me said it was the intention at Washington to relieve Howard and give me command of the Department. I do not believe this, but if true it will not be done now when they find I can't take the field on horse back (keep this to yourself). This is a miserable place, about as large as Vancouver. There are two hotels. I am at the best, called "Hotel de France." I do not know why it is called so except the proprietor and his wife are from France, but there is no French cook, the coffee is awful bad and the bread is worse. I have a good enough room and bed, and they try to do their best. There is or was before the war considerable business done here. It is not a cheerful looking place, located on the banks of the Snake River, a broad rapid stream which empties into the Columbia, surrounded on three sides by tall barren mountains. No timber in sight except a few trees planted in town. It is a terrible dusty place; the wind springs up at ten and lasts till four; there is no such thing as keeping clean. I am sorry I did not bring my old gray suit with me. Time hangs heavy on my hands. I have nothing to do. . . .

I suppose you are lonesome, the post must look forlorn, but you are not more so than I am, and I feel nervous and unsettled all the time. News are daily arriving about movements of Indians and I feel as if I was out of place here. I want to be with the troops and I know they all want me, but I can't ride any distance and I know if I attempt it I should break down and have to come back, which would look worse. All I am fit for is the retired list and the sooner I get there the better. The last news from Howard he was on one side of the river, "The Salmon" and the Indians on the other. They fired a few shots at the troops and told them to come on. The troops have built a raft and expected to cross last night but I do not think the Indians will stand. There may be a skirmish and they will retreat. This I think, but most people here do not agree with me. . . .

A courier came at three this morning from Howard. They had nearly all crossed the river but the Indians had disappeared. He had scouts out hunting for them. He sent through me a telegraph to Washington asking for another Regiment of Infantry to be sent out. This is what I have been urging him to do. He suggests to me if I would like it to form a district of all this country and give me command, Headquarters here, but I don't like it as it would keep me here all summer. If I could get a house here and move you and Anne would go with you I would not mind it so much to stay here till October. Provisions of all sorts are here plenty and cheap. But I have no ambition for any such command. . . .

Indians at the Agency report that the hostiles have recrossed the Salmon River and are making their way towards Canada, where I expected they would go. If this is true they are only thirty miles from here. On the strength of this many reports are floating about town. One is that the Indians have been seen at a lake eighteen miles from here and the last that a farmhouse eight miles off is burning. The citizens are somewhat alarmed and the guard of armed citizens around the town is largely increased for the night. But there is not a particle of danger. . . .

The thermometer has been 102° in the shade today. I have been almost melted but it is much cooler tonight and in my shirt sleeves with the door and windows open I can manage to write. They say this is not one of their hottest days; it sometimes goes up to 110°. Though I am hot I have consoled myself with the thought that I am better off than the troops I sent off this morning. I started Capt. Jackson soon after his arrival with one hundred pack mules with provisions for Howard. I don't know where Howard is. His last letter said he was crossing back with the foot troops the Salmon River and intended to concentrate on Cottonwood, 35 miles from here.

Howard's forward patrol under Capt. Stephen C. Whipple, caught up with the Indians at the origin of Cottonwood Creek on July 4. There was a minor skirmish, but Whipple let the Indians get away, whereas with a little more aggressiveness, he might have ended the war right there. He pursued them east along the south bank of the creek, and found their camp on the west bank of the Clearwater River a week later. When the Indians came out to parley, Whipple's men fired at Chief Looking Glass in violation of a flag of truce, and the battle was on. Howard came up just in time to have the Nez Perce cut him off from all water and supplies for three days; his provisions were dangerously low by the time the pack train sent out by Sully arrived. Howard was rescued, but the Indians got away again. Before the end of the month, the Indians were headed directly for Montana, and Howard thought gratefully that they were now out of his jurisdiction. But the War

Department disagreed; he was ordered to continue the chase.

Meanwhile Sully waited. He began to feel useless and unwanted. The fighting, such as it was, was near him, and he was the most experienced Indian fighter around, but he couldn't even ride out to where the action was. He had to content himself with fighting vicariously, predicting what the Indians were going to do and enjoying some satisfaction when he turned out to be right and Howard wrong. Still he waited, hoping for some kind of a reprieve:

> Another hot sweltering day. I am almost melted. My room has the hot sun on it and is as hot as an oven. We had a scare last night. At 12 o'clock I was woke up by a courier with dispatches from the Agency and Boyle at Fort Lapwai saying Joseph showed himself at the agency with over 200 warriors. Everybody fled from the Agency to the Fort and then sent me word they were safe as K. Jackson's Company was there with the rest of the garrison, but they feared they would make a dash on the farms near Lewiston. I had some citizens woke up and mounted and sent word to all the farms to look out. All the rest of the male citizens surrounded my office calling for arms. I gave them some. Women were out on the streets in force, scared to death, asking me if there was any danger. Of course I got no sleep that night and it has been too hot to sleep so I shall return early hoping Joseph will behave himself.

Alfred was too old a campaigner to worry about Chief Joseph and a few hundred Nez Perce who might raid small towns or settlements. He allayed the fears of the townsfolk and went back to bed.

> I could not sleep last night. My bed was too good. I missed my hard dirty pillow. I expect however I will get used to it and do better in a night or two. . . . Howard is or was July 6th the date I got the last letter from him still on the other side of

227

the Salmon and could not cross. Joe had destroyed all the boats.
He writes me he has to march back to the place he started from
to see if he can cross there. In the meantime Joe is touring
around the country going where he pleases with no one to stop
him. . . . I am now building boats of canvas to be carried on
mules for the troops.

He knew instinctively what was to be in Howard's dispatches
almost before he opened them. Howard was playing cat and
mouse with Chief Joseph, and Joseph was outrunning him. Meanwhile Sully lived in a sweat box and prayed for the day he could
get back to Sophia and his children at Fort Vancouver.

The weather is now pleasant but the hotel is not so pleasant
as it was. All of the women wives of the employees at the
Agency are here with their children, and they occupy rooms on
my floor. I have to keep the door open all day and the noise is
not pleasant. One big woman with specks on has two daughters
about ten years old opposite. She snores and when the girls
don't please her she wallops them and they squall. Next door
to me I have a Mexican woman whose husband is in the mines.
When she is not hawking and spitting she is singing and I
think she is of a consumptive turn. The partitions between the
rooms are so thin you can hear all that is going on in all the
other rooms. She snores too. I suppose I do too when I am
asleep. I am looking for other quarters. There is a small cottage
in the garden where the Clearwater joins the Snake. . . and if the
price is not too high I will hire it as Quartermaster and move
into it. With a Government bunk, a bed sack full of straw and
some blankets I can get along better than here. . .

Howard was having hit-and-run battles with the Indians. Sully
pieced together the reports and played it out like a chess game.
He could predict every move. The Indians took Howard's boats,
and he telegraphed Sully to send some more. Alfred was ready
with them. Howard ran out of supplies and ordered Alfred to

send more through Portland. Sully predicted that army wives would move into Fort Vancouver and admonished Sophia not to let any of them move into her house, "for if you do you will never get rid of them. I am told by those who know that some of them are very vulgar people."

The heat and living conditions, which he would have shrugged off as a younger man, continued to plague him. And the temptation to assume command was always there.

Howard will be in in a few days. They say he wants to leave me in command if I will accept but I don't want it. I think the war is about over. There may still be some skirmishes and long marches, but the thing will quiet down. Joe has had a terrible whipping. He is not the Indian I took him to be for he might have given us much more trouble. This has been the hottest day yet. I have been suffering all day with a headache and neuralgia, but while writing this at 11 P.M. feel much better. A thunder storm is coming over the mountains which has cooled the air. Weeks has planted his blankets in one of our rooms and has been busy killing bats. I think he has killed six. . . Don't be afraid of my being too attentive to the ladies. I feel too miserable to be out sparking and if I did no one would be apt to fall in love with me.

For diversion he made a trip to Walla Walla. Lewiston was getting on his nerves and was rapidly filling up with "negro boys and women all the way from Georgia. They are fast getting places with better wages. Most of the camp women appear to be southern women, 'poor white trash,' and some of them have negro servants."

His Letter of August 26, 1877, reported that he

had a very pleasant time in the boat and reached Walla Walla at 10 Saturday, having travelled all night, but we had to pay for our lunch in the Rail road. Such a road. We left at 2 P.M. and got here about 8 in the evening. The distance about 30 miles. Made four miles an hour on the average. The locomotive about the size of a big tea kettle. Had to stop every few miles when they would fill her up with buckets from the creek and put in a few more sticks to fire her up. We were all packed in freight cars, like cattle, the wind blowing clouds of dust. Babbitt had the bowel complaint and had to ride on a platform car.

Howard continued to hound Joseph's band until they surrendered on October 5. Their surrender did not come as the result of a crushing defeat but because they were under siege; their horses had run away, and they would have had to go through the lines of soldiers to escape. Chief Looking Glass was killed on the last day, and Joseph decided that the cause was hopeless. His band had fought eighteen engagements and won most of them, but most of the warriors had been killed or wounded. When he surrendered at Bear Paws, there were only 87 men, 184 women and 147 children left. The policies of Sherman and Sheridan as executed by Howard had destroyed a nation, at a cost to the government of $1,873,410, not counting individual losses. In addition, those Indians who survived were completely destitute, without even personal possessions, and became wards of the government and a burden on the taxpayers.

Alfred did not have to stay until the bitter end. Three weeks before the surrender he was mercifully sent back to Fort Vancouver, where he finally got a chance to know his wife and children, and to sit in the sun and paint. But his respite was to be short lived. He was dying, and he knew it. For the first time in his life, he sent his sister a letter in which he addressed her by her first name. He wrote to her from Fort Vancouver on April 20, 1879:

Dear Blanche:
Your letter of the 30th of March got here first part of the week. The most interesting news to myself is that I am better than I was last Sunday, but still very sick. I have not been out yet and have got to lie down nearly all day. The fever has left me, but

This is probably the last painting ever done by Alfred. The serenity of the scene was something he savored until his final days.

left me so weak and prostrated that I am used up. The Doctor says I *must* eat meat and rich things to give me strength, but I can't. I have no appetite for anything. The only things I could eat are the things that it is entirely impossible to get, but no doubt that if I did get them I would not want them. It is evident that this is no place for me. I have been here six Summers and every Spring and Summer it is the same thing, only this year it is worse than ever. I have been living in hopes every year that the Regiment would be ordered out, but apparently there is no more prospect now than there was 13 years ago when it first came out. It is usual to move Regiments every four years, but it would cost too much to move us. I am afraid your mortgage for $5,000 is in bad hands and you will lose heavily. It is certain Mr. P — did not see the taxes were too high and there was no lien. How much is the lien for? Never again let him get a mortgage for over 2,000 on any property and never invest without the property is worth at least three times the mortgage. I do not

Sully's paintings grew more somber as he grew older. This self portrait was done when his fighting days were nearing an end.

believe in holding real estate either in New York or Philadelphia. I believe the debt of the city is now 75,000,000 and is increasing as well as taxes. She can never pay that debt and in a few years she and New York will be bankrupt. I sent on $500 to you to deposit in your bank and I don't want to use it, so you can draw on it for what you want until you get out of your trouble. One of the large Ocean steamers is just wrecked at the mouth of the river. All passengers saved, but no baggage and sailors drowned. The Captain still aboard and can't get off. Allie is well. He enjoys himself as I can't hear his lessons. Sophie is well and also the baby. She is quite an amusement for me as I have to be on the bed all day. I started this this afternoon and by writing a little at a time have succeeded in finishing it tonight. All send love.

Yours,
Alf. Sully.

In his last days he finally expressed the love and affection he had held in during his post-California days.

Within three weeks General Alfred Sully was dead. He was given the usual honors of a general officer, and his body was shipped east to be buried in Philadelphia. The eulogies were long and glowing; his career was briefly encapsuled by his friend and commanding officer, General Howard: "May God bless his stricken and mourning family and give them the warmest and most constant of friends among his countrymen, who owe so much of their peace, prosperity, and present liberty and even their national existence to him and such as he. A man who loved duty better than life, and never faltered in the hour of trial."

Howard ordered the flags at all posts in his department flown at half staff and all of the officers at Fort Vancouver to wear a badge of mourning for thirty days, adding this comment: "His service record is already clear and abundant. Let the Army review it, rejoice in it and emulate it, while the old flag floats where he helped to keep it flying."

Afterword

Many historians, when asked to name the country's greatest Indian fighters, fail to list the name of Gen. Alfred Sully, in spite of the facts that, along with Gen. George Crook and Gen. Ranald S. Mackenzie, he was one of our most experienced and successful Indian fighters, and that he fought more Indians in a single battle than any other leader ever met at one time.

Some of the reasons for this error of omission are given in this book: he had an intense dislike for reporters, because he felt that most of them distorted the facts; he had a penchant for speaking his mind and often criticized his superiors; he frequently championed losers or lost causes; by crossing swords with George Armstrong Custer, he came into ill favor with Generals Sheridan and Sherman, the latter being the greatest power in the post–Civil War army; he never published a biography; and he favored a lenient policy toward the Indians rather than the policy of extermination advocated by the War Department.

Two newspaper clippings, found in an old scrapbook kept by Alfred Sully's sisters in Philadelphia, commented on this lack of proper recognition in these succinct words. One said:

> He has never been made famous by letting his men get ambushed or surrounded, and he has not figured therefore in our military annals among those heroes whose celebrity arises from useless sacrifice of themselves or the soldiers under them.

The other remarked, with a sympathy toward Sully that was rare in the press:

> It is a curious commentary upon the caprices of military glory that the government has to take counsel of "Colonel" Sully for the relief of "General" Howard. Sully is an old soldier, who has spent most of his life on the frontier and knows the Indians well. When Howard was playing soldier in the East, Sully was fighting Indians in the West, and having no newspaper correspondents to sing his praises, the public heard little of him and the government forgot him.

Notes

CHAPTER 1.

1. He wrote home: "I suppose they have told you all about my examination, etc., etc., which I thought would be so dreadful, but which was so simple that I would not have troubled myself about it had I known it; but yet my standing in my class is not as good as it should be, which is owing perhaps to my being so bad a Frenchman, or there being so many good Frenchmen in the Class. But I must hope for better luck and try, too."

2. Henry B. Dawson, *Battles of the United States by Sea and Land* (New York: Johnson, Fry, 1858), II, 498.

3. In 1848 a captain in the army got a base pay of $150 a month. As a first lieutenant Alfred received $125 a month plus 10 percent because he had been in the service for more than five years. (*Resolution of the House of Representatives* of August 30, 1842.)

4. There were twenty-two missions between San Diego and San Francisco: San Diego (established July 16, 1769); San Luis Rey (June 13, 1798); San Antonio de Pala (1816); San Juan Capistrano (November 1, 1776); San Gabriel (September 8, 1771); San Fernando Rey (September 8, 1797); San Buenaventura (March 3, 1782); Santa Barbara (December 4, 1786); Santa Inez (September 17, 1804); La Purisima Concepcion (December 8, 1787); San Luis Obispo (September 1, 1772); San Miguel Arcangel (July 25, 1797); San Antonio de Padua (July 14, 1771); Nuestra de la Soledad (October 9, 1791); San Carlos Borromeo del Carmelo (June 3, 1770); San Juan Bautista (June 25, 1797); Santa Cruz (September 25, 1791); Santa Clara (January 12, 1777); San Jose de Guadalupe (June 11, 1797); San Francisco de Asís, or Dolores (October 9, 1776); San Rafael Arcangel (December 14, 1817), and San Francisco Solano de Sonoma (July 4, 1823). The original plan was to space them about thirty miles apart so that a traveler could go from one to the next in a day, although in the completed plan there was some variation. Travelers were welcome to eat and sleep at no cost, as they were at most California ranchos while Alfred was there. The missions provided wheat, barley, corn, beans, and peas as well as apricots, melons, olives, oranges, peaches, pears, plums, and grapes. Meat was plentiful; Mission San Luis Rey in 1832 had 27,500 head of cattle and eleven other missions at various times counted over 10,000 head each. The mission fathers not only fed the Indians well but taught them about fifty trades including tanning, weaving, carpentry, tile-making, and stone-cutting. [Maynard Geiger, O.F.M., *A Brief History of the Mission Period* (Santa Barbara: Franciscan Brothers, 1947.)]

5. Allan Nevins and Henry Steele Commager, *A Pocket History of the United States* (New York: Washington Square Press, 1967), pp. 189–190; also Hubert Howe Bancroft, *History of California* (Santa Barbara: Wallace Hebbard, 1969), IV, 351, 365.
6. *Ibid.*
7. *Ibid.*
8. *Ibid.*
9. *Ibid.*
10. The building still stands today. It has been beautifully remodeled and houses a fine museum, but it still looks much as Alfred pictured it in his watercolors when he first arrived in Monterey.
11. Five of the seven officers who went after the deserters became generals in the Civil War: William T. Sherman, Nelson H. Davis, E. R. S. Canby, Alfred Gibbs, and Alfred Sully. [Sources: William T. Sherman, *Memoirs of William T. Sherman* (New York: D. Appleton, 1875), I, 71; the Sully letters; Bvt. Maj. Gen. George W. Cullum, *Biographical Register of the Officers and Graduates of the United States Military Academy* (New York: D. Van Nostrand, 1868), I, 590, 595 and II, 27, 168, 174. Hereafter referred to as Cullum, *Biographical Register.*]
12. Nelson H. Davis entered West Point the year Alfred graduated, but he was with Sully at Veracruz and sailed around the Horn with him. After they left Monterey, they went separate ways, but Davis was present at most of the same battles as Alfred during the Civil War, only he was assistant inspector general. He was in several skirmishes against the Apache Indians in Arizona, but most of his military career was spent in locating posts, conducting special investigations, and exploring the country.
13. Henry W. Halleck was professor of engineering at West Point while Alfred was there. At the time Alfred mentions him, he was serving as secretary of state of California. He resigned his commission in 1854 but rejoined the army when the Civil War broke out. As a major general he commanded all of the army operations in the West during Sully's last year there and was general in chief of the Armies of the United States from July 11, 1862, to March 12, 1864, when he became chief of staff. (Cullum, *Biographical Register*, I, 573.)
14. Doña Angustias was only two years older than Alfred.
15. The army consisted of cavalry (horse soldiers), infantry (foot soldiers), and dragoons (soldiers who fought either on horseback or afoot).
16. The convention met in Colton Hall, a schoolhouse built by Walter Colton, who was alcade at Monterey from 1846 to 1848 and editor and publisher (with Robert Semple) of *The Californian*, the first newspaper in California, in 1846 and 1847. The building has been slightly modified but remains basically the same today as it was then. It is open to the public as a tourist attraction.

CHAPTER 2.
1. While the missions have lost their herds and their fields, most of their chapels have been maintained or restored and still serve as parish churches or tourist attractions.
2. Sarah Sully was fond of all animals, but especially fond of dogs. This is best illustrated by an item taken from the *Philadelphia Enquirer* in the late 1800s:
"Some years ago, Mrs. Sully, the wife of the late lamented artist, had a pointer to

whom she was much attached. Ponto, her constant companion, was greatly attached to his mistress, and we might fill a volume with an account of his many interesting exploits but shall content ourselves with one. On one occasion he met a couple of half-starved dogs in the street and brought them to the back gate opening into Mrs. Sully's yard, where he presented them to his mistress. He could not speak, but if pantomime meant anything, he distinctly said: 'My dear, good, charitable mistress, here are two starved friends of mine who want something to eat!' The appeal was not in vain, and they departed after having been supplied with a good meal. This was the commencement of Mrs. Sully's charity visitors, and any person might witness the daily occurrence of some six or seven dogs, at a certain hour, presenting themselves at that estimable lady's gate for the purpose of receiving their rations. This best of women, whose heart and hand were ever open, responsive to the slightest murmur of distress, was in the habit of cooking a large meal daily for her canine callers, as she did not approve of giving them raw meat, and to visitors at the house the odor of the culinary arrangements was always painfully perceptible." Alfred shared his mother's love for dogs and his sketch books are filled with studies of various breeds in different poses.

CHAPTER 3.
1. Tredwell Moore had graduated from West Point in 1847, came around Cape Horn at the same time Alfred did; he was Sully's assistant quartermaster. He remained in the Quartermaster Department for almost his entire military career.
2. The theatre was actually a saloon owned by Jack Swan, an English sailor who had arrived in 1843. Alfred and some of his fellow officers persuaded Swan to convert part of it to a theatre. The first performance, *"Putnam, The Lion of '76,"* packed the 150-seat house at five dollars a head. When audiences dwindled because of the gold rush, performances were given free of charge. William Randolph Hearst bought the theatre in 1906 and turned it over to the city of Monterey with the proviso that it become an historical landmark. (*Monterey Peninsula Herald*, June 1, 1970.)
3. Father Romano Ramirez de Arellno, the Dominican priest who married Alfred and Manuela was reprimanded by the Church and recalled in February 1853. [Rev. Zephyrin Englehart, O.F.M., *Missions and Missionaries* (published by the Franciscan Fathers of California, 1915), IV, 692.]
4. Elias K. Kane, a member of Alfred's class at West Point, was behind Sully academically but outranked him. Kane was in the dragoons while Alfred was in the infantry, and promotions were less frequent in the infantry. Kane died while on leave of absence in 1853; he was thirty-three years old.
5. David R. Jones also sailed around Cape Horn at the same time Sully did and served with him in Monterey and Benicia. When the Civil War broke out he joined the Southern states and died in Richmond at the age of thirty-nine.
6. Don Manuel sent two of his sons, Antonio and Porfirio, back east when Lt. William T. Sherman offered to take them there and put them in school. [Hubert Howe Bancroft, *History of California* (Santa Barbara: Wallace Hebbard, 1969), IV, 692.]
7. The Convent of Santa Catalina was established next door to the Jimeno house by the Order of St. Dominico.

8. James L. Ord came to California as a surgeon under a contract with the army but was not an army man. When Manuel Jimeno died in 1853, Dr. Ord married his widow, Doña Angustias. In spite of Alfred's vituperative remarks about him at the time of Manuela's death, they apparently became good friends, for in 1861 Ord wrote to Sully: "Captain, if you come on! I have some of the best Pear Brandy perhaps to make the best hot punches that you ever drank; now it's three years old. Will keep a dozen bottles for your special benefit if you will promise to come on soon. It will bring back the natural color of your hair, take all of the wrinkles out of your face and make you as good looking and as jovial as Falstaff ever was. From accidentally being thrown from a horse some three years since I cannot drink too much, but can and am making a good collection of choice liquors for those who do. Tonight Miss Orena, the Doña's youngest sister, gives a "Grand Balle" . . . wish you were here to enjoy it. It would remind you of olden times . . . which is very pleasant to bring back to our memory, especially as we are getting old and will soon have to fall back on the past to refresh ourselves with happy thoughts."

9. The author and his wife made two trips to Monterey doing research on this book; on each occasion we searched for the grave of Manuela. The first search was written up by Mayo Hayes O'Donnell in the *Monterey Peninsula Herald* (July 15, 1955) and as a result one of her readers claimed to have found it. On the second trip, many years later, Harry Downie told us where it was. But we still could not locate it.

CHAPTER 4

1. The de la Guerra House is now El Paseo, one of the more elegant restaurant-shop complexes in Santa Barbara. Don Jose had not only the fine house that Alfred describes, but behind it he built a wheat mill and an olive oil mill; a bakery; a tannery; metal shops for making kitchen utensils and farm implements; silver-smith shops; places for weaving, making cheese, wines, candles and everything else that his large household needed or wanted. The house was built by three thousand Indians. For years they had been under his paternalistic care sharing the largess from his farms. Every year he had been in the habit of sending them away with provisions for a two weeks excursion. But one year only fifteen hundred of the three thousand went on the trip. Saying nothing, the other fifteen hundred stayed behind and began to build the house on the site he had selected, using materials they had made themselves as well as timbers, wood and hardware he had imported from Spain. At the end of a week the fifteen hundred Indians who had been away returned and took over for those who had remained behind to work. The house was completed in two weeks and had adobe walls that were six feet thick. Don Jose paid his help in food, clothing and shelter; they had no need for money. But he kept $250,000 in gold in a tower in his house. This was used to buy the cargo he wanted from any ship that touched port, and his was the first port of call for the captain of any ship that came into the harbor. He also lent money to the ships' supercargoes to pay customs duties and to the rancheros who needed it; from the latter he received cattle in exchange for gold. [Sources: Elizabeth Style Madison, "Hacienda de la Guerra y Noriega" (*Sunset Magazine*, January 1911), pp. 37–47; William Heath Davis, *Seventy Five*

Years in California (San Francisco: Howell, 1967), pp. 184–186.]

2. Jose de la Guerra y Noriega was born in Spain in 1775 and was a captain in the Spanish army; as such he spent some time in Mexico. When Mexico severed her ties with Spain he resigned his commission and went to Santa Barbara to represent the Mexican government. He already had land grants from the king of Spain and in Santa Barbara he added to his immense wealth. He owned Las Positas Rancho, twelve leagues; Simi Rancho, fourteen leagues; Callegua Rancho, five leagues; El Conejo Rancho, three leagues, and San Julian Rancho, eleven leagues. These ranchos had about twenty thousand head of cattle and eight thousand horses. In addition he had vast vineyards. He was known as the patriarch of California, being called upon to settle many local and family disputes even after he had resigned his official position, and his charities were legend. He had four daughters and five sons and left more than a hundred direct descendents. His sons succeeded in squandering most of his fortune even before his death in 1858. (Bancroft, *History of California*, III, 469–471.)

3. Maria Teresa married William E. P. Hartnell, a successful merchant. They had twenty sons and five daughters; in his later years Hartnell took to drink and lost most of his money. (Bancroft, *History of California*, III, 777–778.) Anna Maria married Dr. Alfred Robinson, who was also a successful businessman. Doña Angustias married Dr. James Ord after the death of her first husband, Don Manuel Jimeno by whom she had eleven children. (Bancroft, IV, 692.) Maria Antonia married Cesario Lataillade, a well-known and successful businessman who was vice consul of Spain at Monterey, although he lived in Santa Barbara; in 1849 he accidentally shot and killed himself. His widow married Gaspar Orena, a wealthy Spanish trader who lived in Santa Barbara.

4. On another occasion Thomas Sully promised Alfred that he would paint a religious picture as a present for the Doña. He knew that she was a devout Catholic and thought such a gift might please her. But months passed and the picture did not arrive. Then one day a man walking along the beach found a box that had been washed ashore from a vessel which had been wrecked further up the coast. The crate was addressed to Don Manuel and when it was opened there was a tin box containing a life-sized painting of "Christ Blessing Little Children." The picture was not damaged and even though it was unsigned, Alfred identified it as the work of his father. The author and his wife have located the missing painting by Thomas Sully in the private home of a wealthy family in Santa Barbara. The owners do not wish their names divulged for fear that they will be besieged by the critic, the art lover, or the just plain curious.

5. In his will he wrote: "Although my present wife has sufficient property, I have not at the present time received any of it, the same being entrusted by me to her father with whom she still lives. The property which I possess is mine exclusively and I have acquired it by working for it myself. At the time I married my present wife in the year 1833, I perhaps had a capital of about $20,000 and whatever exceeds that amount now are profits obtained during the period of our married life and I remark, though with sorrow, and only impelled by the force of truth with which I must now speak, that in as much as it is public

and notorious in California that my brother-in-law without my authority, sometimes and most of the times with my wife's authorization, disposed arbitrarily and without my consent of a considerable portion of my property as they saw fit, and this being the real cause of my coming to this Capitol in order that I might save myself from those extortions of which facts both my brother, The Rev. Father Fray Antonio Jimeno and my executor have full knowledge, and upon whom I would urge that they constantly bear in mind at the time of the division and distribution of the property acquired during our married life, which property was the cause of those unpleasant disagreements. I make this declaration so that everybody will know it."

6. Thomas Sully rarely wrote to Alfred, but when he did it was usually to assure Alfred that he had enough money to get by on and did not need any help. Before his son had left for California, Thomas had written: "Your letter enclosing a draft on New York for 150 was duly received; and though I know Rosalie has answered it, I must say a few words on the subject.

"I have a suspicion that you thought I was so pressed that this small sum would be an aid for the present—Thank Heaven I am not so hard run; but yet I feel as warm a thrill of gratitude for your manly effort as if I had needed it. I have deposited it in the Farmer and Mechanics' Bank for collection in New York and safekeeping, and where it will be ready for you when you require it. But I beg you will spare all you can from your necessary expenses and send it to me that I may add to it and it will prove a serviceable friend when you need it." Alfred continued to follow this advice as long as his father was alive.

"I will give you a general account of how I stand at present," the letter continues, "from which you will perceive that with all my management, I shall be able to save a small pittance for your sisters when I die; but they will have to depend chiefly on their own industry for support. . . .

"I have an insurance on my life for $1,000 and property in paintings, at least worth one more—Thus you are in possession of all my expectancies. . . .

"In the meantime I owe not one dollar, and have a few hundred lying in the bank for any exigency. Add to these good things the blessing of excellent health, and troops of friends, and I think I have no right to complain.

"At your time of life this statement is due. When I go, your sisters will depend upon you and your brother for advice and confidence, and I feel confident that they will not be disappointed."

Thomas Sully, Jr., Alfred's brother, died four years after this letter was written, but his father lived on for more than thirty years.

CHAPTER 5

1. Col. Charles F. Smith had been president of the Board of Claims for supplies furnished to the California Volunteers by Col. John C. Frémont. Frémont was given an unusually generous allowance for his supplies and was later convicted of misappropriation of government funds on another count. [Bvt. Maj. Gen. George W. Cullum, *Biographical Register of the Officers and Graduates of the United States Military Academy* (New York: D. Van Nostrand, 1868), I, 280.]

2. Hubert Howe Bancroft, *History of California* (Santa Barbara: Wallace Hebbard, 1969), VI, 473.

3. *Ibid.*

4. *Ibid.*

5. Up to this point Hannibal Day's career had not been a glorious one. His first ten years as an officer were spent in garrison duty at Fort Brady, Michigan; Fort Niagara, New York, and Fort Dearborn, Illinois, with three years sandwiched in on topographical duty. He was in the Black Hawk expedition in 1832, "but not at the seat of the war." He was in Hancock Barracks, Maine, from 1833–36; Fort Independence, Massachusetts, in 1836, and then on recruiting duty for two years. He finally got into the Florida War in 1838 but was on sick leave from 1839–41. He turned up briefly at the close of the Seminole Indian War, was in one battle in the war with Mexico (Tampico), and then spent the rest of his time until the Civil War on either garrison duty or frontier duty. During the first six months of the Civil War, he was in Georgetown and spent the next year and a half on recruiting service. He was finally sent into battle at Gettysburg in command of a brigade but retired from active service a month later "on his own application." He was made a brevet brigadier general "for long and faithful services in the army." (Cullum, *Biographical Register*, I, 250.)

6. Frederick Steele had fought in a number of battles in the war with Mexico and after his tour of duty in California served on frontier duty until the War between the States. Here he served with distinction and was made a brevet major general. (*Ibid.*, II, 92.)

7. Thomas Wright left California in 1854 but after three years of frontier duty died at the age of twenty-nine. (*Ibid.*, II, 240.)

8. Garrison duty, frontier and recruiting service made drunkards out of many an army man. Albert S. Miller had spent about twenty years in this type of service. (*Ibid.*, I, 255.)

9. Bancroft, *History of California*, VI, 453.

10. Yreka was a thriving mining town on the northern tip of California.

11. J. P. Dunn, Jr., *Massacres of the Mountains* (first published in 1886. Reprinted, New York: Archer House, c. 1965), p. 171.

12. Edmund Russell was a West Point graduate (class of 1846) who had seen action in the Mexican War and been at Benicia with the Fourth Infantry while Alfred was there. He was killed in California near Red Bluffs on March 24, 1853. (Cullum, *Biographical Register*, II, 178.)

13. Bradford Alden's story is a particularly sad one. Fourteen of his sixteen years as an officer at West Point were spent as an instructor and commandant of cadets for the Military Academy. Sick of this duty, he handed in his resignation. Before it could be acted upon, he was sent to the West Coast. Here he was severely wounded in action on August 24, 1853, and was partially paralyzed on one side. His resignation was accepted. When the Civil War broke out he offered his services to the Union but was rejected because of the disability he had suffered at the Rogue River. In the meantime he had bored forty-six oil wells in western Pennsylvania. (Cullum, *Biographical Register*, I, 393.)

14. Dunn, *Massacres of the Mountains*, p. 175.

15. Fairfax Downey, *Indian Wars of the U.S. Army 1776–1865* (New York: Doubleday, 1963), p. 179.

16. The journal and the watercolor illustrations were auctioned off in New York about forty years ago; all efforts to locate them have been futile.

CHAPTER 6.

1. William Addelman Ganoe, *History of the United States Army* (New York: D. Appleton–Century, 1942), p. 234.

2. General Orders #2, Headquarters of the Army, New York, September 26, 1853.

3. *Returns from Regular Army Regiments*. National Archives Microfilm Publication M665, roll 19, January 1854 to December 1860.

4. Engaged in the Powder River campaign at the time Sully was fighting Indians in the Northwest, Cols. Nelson Cole and Samuel Walker had 514 horses freeze to death in 36 hours. [Robert M. Utley, *Frontiersmen in Blue* (New York: Macmillan, 1967), pp. 329–330.]

5. Ganoe, *History of the United States Army*, p. 230.

6. *Ibid.*, p. 244.

7. Louis M. Roddis, *The Indian Wars of Minnesota* (Cedar Rapids, Torch Press, 1956), p. 19.

8. *Ibid.*

9. William R. Montgomery had served with distinction in the Mexican War but was dismissed from the service for "appropriating a portion of the military reserve at Fort Riley, Kansas, to the uses of the Pawnee Association for a townsite, he being interested in that association. Dismissed December 8, 1855." [Bvt. Maj. Gen. George W. Cullum, *Biographical Register of the Officers and Graduates of the United States Military Academy* (New York: D. Van Nostrand, 1868), I, 284.]

10. William S. Harney, then a colonel, gained dubious fame in the Seminole Indian War when he was literally caught with his pants down during an Indian raid and had to swim a river to safety in his underwear. Harney went on to become a grim, tough fighter who neither asked for nor gave any quarter. During the Black Hawk War when the Indians wanted to talk truce at the Battle of Bad Axe, Harney participated in the slaughter of between 150 and 300 Indians, including women and children. At Ash Hollow on the North Platte River he went through the formality of demanding that the Indians surrender some of their warriors who had participated in the Grattan Massacre, then promptly pushed the Indians into a trap and murdered eighty-six of them. [Fairfax Downey, *Indian Wars of the U.S. Army 1776–1865* (New York: Doubleday, 1963), pp. 128, 135, 186.]

The Grattan Massacre occurred when an Indian shot and butchered a straying sick cow. John L. Grattan, who had graduated from West Point only the year before (1853) was anxious to show his fighting ability and received permission to go into a camp of 1,000 Sioux warriors to arrest the culprit. When the Sioux refused to give the man up and insisted that the matter be settled when the annuities were paid, Grattan opened fire on them with a twelve-pound howitzer and a twelve-pound mountain gun. The Indians killed his entire force of twenty-seven men. (Utley, *Frontiersmen in Blue,* pp. 113–114.)

11. The trouble at Ash Hollow developed because an Indian shot an old, wornout cow abandoned by its Mormon owner. The Mormon demanded twenty-five dollars in payment; the Indians offered ten. When the owner called for a punitive detail, Harney killed 86 Indians, wounded 5 and captured about 70 women and children at Ash Hollow just north of the North Platte River, on September 3, 1855. These were supposedly friendly Indians.

12. Robert G. Athearn, *Forts of the Upper Missouri* (Englewood Cliffs, N.J.: Prentice-Hall, 1967), p. 38.

13. Alfred's second wife, Sophia, was aware of the relationships between soldiers and Indians of the Sioux tribes on the frontier. She refused to let her husband hang the picture of the Indian girls in her house.

CHAPTER 7.

1. U.S. Department of Commerce, Bureau of the Census, *Historical Statistics of the United States, Colonial Times to 1957,* 2nd ed. (Washington, D.C.: Government Printing Office, 1961), p. 66.

2. Samuel R. Curtis's career up to that point was a spotty one. After a taste of frontier duty he resigned from the army one year after he was graduated from West Point in 1831. He became a civil engineer and an attorney in Ohio, but as a colonel in the Ohio militia joined with his unit in the Mexican War where he spent two years guarding military supplies and serving as governor and commandant of Camargo, and as civil and military governor of Saltillo, Mexico. He resigned as soon as he could and worked as a civil engineer and an attorney, being elected to the U.S. House of Representatives from Iowa, 1857 to 1861. He was on the Committee on Military Affairs during that time. When the war broke out he was appointed colonel of the Second Regiment, Iowa Volunteers, June 1, 1861. Strangely enough, he was appointed a brigadier general two weeks before he was named a colonel. He was in a number of minor skirmishes but only one major battle, Pea Ridge, Arkansas; nevertheless he served temporarily as commander of the Department of the Missouri and commander of the Department of Kansas. [Bvt. Maj. Gen. George W. Cullum, *Biographical Register of the Officers and Graduates of the United States Military Academy* (New York: D. Van Nostrand, 1868), I, 395.]

3. The charges were brought by Frank Blair, one of the most influential men in Missouri. But he was not as influential as Senator Benton, Frémont's father-in-law. (Edwin C. McReynolds, *Missouri: A History of the Crossroads State* (Norman: University of Oklahoma, 1962), p. 237.

4. William Addelman Ganoe, *History of the United States Army* (New York: D. Appleton–Century, 1942), pp. 246–247.

5. *Ibid.,* p. 248.

6. In the twenty-three years he had been in the army since graduating from West Point, McDowell had had only one day in combat and on that occasion he was serving as an adjutant. (Cullum, *Biographical Register,* I, 559.)

7. Ganoe, *History of the United States Army,* p. 253.

8. *Ibid.*

9. Staff officers—major and above—rode on horseback; line officers—captain and below—marched on foot.

CHAPTER 8.

1. T. Harry Williams, *Lincoln and His Generals* (New York: Alfred Knopf, 1952), p. 70.

2. *Ibid.*, p. 84.

3. Maj. Gen. Alexander S. Webb, *The Peninsula* (New York: Charles Scribner's Sons, 1881), pp. 18, 23.

4. *Ibid.*, p. 36.

5. *Ibid.*

6. According to my parents, Sully is reputed to have ordered his men to shoot any soldier who turned his back on the enemy.

7. Gen. Silas Casey was a seasoned combat soldier, having been in the Seminole Indian War, the war with Mexico, and in skirmishes with the Indians while on frontier duty. At Fair Oaks his Second Division was on the front line facing the Confederates who were attacking from the southwest. Casey had three brigades: the first was on the right under Brig. Gen. Henry M. Naglee, who had been in and out of the army three times since he had graduated from West Point so that he had only three years of service since he had left the Military Academy, and those three years were on three separate and unrelated tours of duty; the second, in the center, was under the command of Brig. Gen. Henry W. Wessels, who had been with Sully in the Seminole War, the War with Mexico, and on frontier duty as Alfred's senior officer, and Sully felt that he was a superior combat soldier; the third brigade, on the left, was under Brig. Gen. Innis N. Palmer who had been a cavalry officer since he had graduated from West Point in 1846 and had led infantry troops in battle only once, at Williamsburg, less than a month before the battle of Fair Oaks. Behind Casey's division was that of Gen. Darius N. Couch whose combat experience had been limited to three days, aside from some skirmishes in the War in Florida. Casey's strength was in Wessels, who was in the center of the front line. Palmer's troops were raw, untrained, "in a poor state of discipline" and unable to be controlled by their officers. It was here that the rebels hit first, and the men broke with a loss of about 25 percent as contrasted to Wessels's loss of only 34 men killed and 271 wounded out of a brigade of 1,500. Having broken the brigade on the left side, the rebels attacked Abercrombie on the right, hitting him from the front and flank, and driving him back into Couch's division in the rear. The North was on the verge of defeat, and for his part Casey would be assigned to the command of the supply depot at the White House. (Webb, *The Peninsula*, pp. 101–105.)

8. Bruce Catton, *Terrible Swift Sword* (New York: Doubleday, 1963), p. 313.

9. *Ibid.*, p. 314.

10. A regiment consisted of about one thousand men; a brigade of four or more regiments and a division of three or more brigades. However, these units were rarely if ever at full strength due to desertions, killed, wounded, and missing combined with a lack of replacements. For example, Wessels's brigade at Fair Oaks numbered only fifteen hundred men.

11. Williams, *Lincoln and His Generals*, p. 177.

12. Carl Sandburg, *Abraham Lincoln: The War Years* (New York: Harcourt Brace, 1939), I, 532.

13. *Terrible Swift Sword*, p. 452.

14. Sandburg, *Abraham Lincoln: The War Years*, I, 551.

15. *Ibid.*, p. 629.

16. *Ibid.*

CHAPTER 9.

1. From the Sully papers.

2. Louis M. Roddis, *The Indian Wars of Minnesota* (Cedar Rapids: Torch Press, 1956), p. 97.

3. *Ibid.*, p. 84.

4. Herbert M. Hart, *Old Forts of the Northwest, 1850–1890* (Seattle: Superior, 1963), p. 119.

5. William Watts Folwell, *A History of Minnesota* (St. Paul: Minnesota Historical Society, 1961), II, 124.

6. Geraldine Bean, "General Sully and the Northwest Indian Expedition," *North Dakota History*, XXXIII, no. 3 (Summer 1966): 245.

7. *Ibid.*

8. *Ibid.*, p. 246.

9. Evan Jones, *The Minnesota: Forgotten River* (New York: Holt, Rinehart and Winston, 1962), p. 84.

10. U.S. War Department, *The War of the Rebellion: A Compilation of the Official Records of the Union and Confederate Armies*, series I (Washington, D.C.: Government Printing Office, 1880–1901, XXII: 350. Hereafter cited as *O.R.*

11. Bean, "General Sully and the Northwest Indian Expedition," *North Dakota History*, p. 249.

12. Folwell, *History of Minnesota*, II, 183.

13. C. M. Oehler, *The Great Sioux Uprising* (New York: Oxford University, 1959), p. 140; also Folwell, *History of Minnesota*, II: 176.

14. Oehler, pp. 136–141.

15. *Ibid.*, pp. 133, 136–139, 141.

16. *O.R.*, 22: 463.

17. *Ibid.*, pp. 496–497.

18. Most of Sully's quotations regarding his Indian campaigns are taken from his official reports and documents, and thus lack the personal touch found in his letters.

19. "No other military commander, either before or since, so fully and completely, yet so humanely, chastised and subdued the Sioux bands." (Dr. DeLorme W. Robinson, "Editorial Notes on Historical Sketch of North and South Dakota," *South Dakota Historical Collections*, vol. 1, 1902.)

20. From the Sully papers on loan to the Huntington Library.

21. *Ibid.*

22. *Ibid.*; also Bean, "General Sully and the Northwest Indian Expedition," *North Dakota History*, p. 249.

CHAPTER 10.

1. From the Sully papers.

2. From a paper prepared by Col. M. T. Thomas of the Eighth Volunteer Regiment.

3. *Ibid.*

4. He assigned Colonel Dill, with six companies of the Thirtieth Wisconsin, to construct and man the fort. [John Barness and William Dickinson, "The Sully Expedition of 1864," *Montana Western History*, XVI, no. 3 (Summer 1966).]

5. *Ibid.*

6. From the diary of L. K. Raymond, Company I, Third Illinois Cavalry, "Trip Over the Plains of Dakota in 1865," *North Dakota Historical Society Quarterly*, II, no. 3 (1928).

7 Sully and Thomas apparently had a good relationship even though Sully was not enthusiastic about militia officers. He had enough confidence in Thomas to let him assume command of a major battle. Thomas, in turn, wrote of Sully that although he "was rather past the vigorous days of the prime of manhood, his perceptions were remarkably clear, and he appeared to know intuitively just where the Indians were and what they would do. These instinctive qualities—fully developed by long service in the regular army—rendered him more fully competent for the duty to which he had been assigned, and, added to these, a genial temperament made him an agreeable commander."

8. John Barness and William Dickinson, "The Sully Expedition of 1864," *Montana Western History*, XVI, no. 3 (Summer 1966): 28.

9. *Ibid.*

10. *Ibid.*

11. *Ibid.*

12. Herbert M. Hart, *Old Forts of the Northwest, 1850–1890* (Seattle: Superior, 1963).

CHAPTER 12.

1. Robert M. Utley, *Frontiersmen in Blue* (New York: Macmillan, 1967), p. 308.

2. *Ibid.*, p. 310.

3. *Ibid.*

4. *Ibid.*, pp. 317, 333–334.

5. *Ibid.*, p. 336.

6. From the Sully papers.

7. General Order #23, War Department, Adjutant General's Office, April 10, 1866.

8. George A. Custer, *My Life on the Plains,* ed. Milton Quaife (Lakeside Press, 1952).

9. *Ibid.*

10. Alvin Josephy, Jr., *The Nez Perce Indians and the Opening of the Northwest* (New Haven: Yale University, 1965).

11. *Ibid.*

12. Helen Addison Howard and Dan L. McGrath, *War Chief Joseph* (Caldwell, Idaho: Caxton, 1941).

13. *Ibid.*

Bibliography

Athearn, Robert G. *Forts of the Upper Missouri*. Englewood Cliffs, N.J.: Prentice-Hall, 1967.

Atherton, Gertrude. *The Splendid Idle Forties*. New York: Grosset & Dunlap, 1902.

Bancroft, Hubert Howe. *History of California*, vols. III, IV, and VI. San Francisco: History Company, 1886; reprinted Santa Barbara, Calif.: Wallace Hebbard, 1969.

Bancroft, Hubert Howe. *History of Oregon*, vols. I and II. New York: McGraw, 1967.

Barness, John and Dickinson, William. "The Sully Expedition of 1864." *Montana Western History*, XVI, no. 3 (Summer 1966).

Bean, Geraldine. "General Sully and the Northwest Indian Expedition." *North Dakota History Magazine*, XXXIII, no. 3 (Summer 1966).

Bolton, Herbert E. *The Spanish Borderlands*. New Haven: Yale University, 1921.

Brooks, Chester L. and Mattison, Ray H. *Theodore Roosevelt and the Badlands*. Washington, D.C.: U.S. Department of the Interior, National Park Services, 1958.

Brown, Dee. *Fort Phil Kearny: An American Saga*. New York: G. P. Putnam's Sons, 1962.

Catton, Bruce. *Mr. Lincoln's Army*. New York: Doubleday, 1951.

————. *Never Call Retreat*. New York: Doubleday, 1965.

————. *Stillness at Appomattox*. New York: Doubleday, 1953.

————. *Terrible Swift Sword*. New York: Doubleday, 1963.

————. *This Hallowed Ground*. New York: Doubleday, 1956.

Cleland, Robert Glass. *From Wilderness to Empire*. New York: Alfred A. Knopf, 1959.

Colton, Rev. Walter. *Three Years in California*. New York: A. S. Barnes & Burr, 1860.

Congdon, Don. *Combat: The Civil War*. New York: Dell, 1967.

Croghan, Col. George. *Army Life on the Western Frontier*. Norman: University of Oklahoma, 1958.

Crook, Gen. George. *Autobiography*. Norman: University of Oklahoma, 1946.

Cullum, Bvt. Maj. Gen. George W. *Biographical Register of the Officers and Graduates of the United States Military Academy*. New York: D. Van Nostrand, 1868.

Cunningham, Frank. *General Stand Watie's Confederate Indians*. San Antonio: Naylor, 1959.

Custer, George A. *My Life on the Plains*. Edited by Milton Quaife. Lakeside Press, 1952.

Dana, Richard Henry, Jr. *Two Years Before the Mast*. Boston: James R. Osgood, 1877.

BIBLIOGRAPHY

Davis, William Heath. *Seventy Five Years in California*. San Francisco: Howell, 1967.

Dawson, Henry B. *Battles of the United States by Sea and Land*, vol. II. New York: Johnson, Fry, 1858.

Del Rey, Lester. *A Pirate Flag for Monterey*. Canada: John C. Winston, 1952.

Doubleday, Abner. *Chancellorsville and Gettysburg*. New York: Charles Scribner's Sons, 1882.

Downey, Fairfax. *Indian Wars of the U.S. Army 1776–1865*. New York: Doubleday, 1963.

Dunn, J. P., Jr. *Massacres of the Mountains: A History of the Indians of the Far West 1815–1875*. New York: Archer House, c. 1965.

Englehart, Rev. Zephyrin, O.F.M. *Missions and Missionaries*, vol. IV. Published by the Franciscan Fathers of California, 1915.

Finerty, John F. *War-path and Bivouac: Or, Big Horn and Yellowstone Expedition*. Chicago: Lakeside Press, 1955.

Folwell, William Watts. *A History of Minnesota*, vol. II. St. Paul: Minnesota Historical Society, 1961.

Ganoe, William Addelman. *The History of the United States Army*. New York: D. Appleton–Century, 1942.

Geiger, Maynard, O.F.M. *A Brief History of the Mission Period*. Santa Barbara, Calif., 1947.

Grant, U. S. *Personal Memoirs*. New York: Charles S. Webster, 1885.

Hart, Herbert M. *Old Forts of the Northwest, 1850–1890*. Seattle: Superior, 1963.

————. *Pioneer Forts of the West*. Seattle: Superior, 1968.

Hill, Laurance L. *Santa Barbara, Tierra Adora*. Los Angeles: Security First National Bank, 1930.

Howard, Helen Addison and McGrath, Dan L. *War Chief Joseph*. Caldwell, Idaho: Caxton, 1941.

Howarth, David. *Panama*. New York: McGraw-Hill, 1966.

Johnson, R. W. *War Memories* (a lecture delivered February 28, 1888, at the Young Men's Christian Association, Northfield, Minn.).

Jones, Evan. *The Minnesota: Forgotten River*. New York: Holt, Rinehart and Winston, 1962.

Josephy, Alvin, Jr. *The Nez Perce Indians and the Opening of the Northwest*. New Haven: Yale University, 1965.

Kantor, MacKinley. *Andersonville*. New York: Signet Books, 1957.

Leckie, William H. *The Military Conquest of the Southern Plains*. Norman: University of Oklahoma, 1963.

Longstreet, Stephen. *Warcries on Horseback*. New York: Doubleday, 1970.

Madison, Elizabeth Style. "Hacienda de la Guerra y Noriega." *Sunset Magazine*, January 1911.

McReynolds, Edwin C. *Missouri: A History of the Crossroads State*. Norman: University of Oklahoma, 1962.

Mitchell, Joseph B. *Decisive Battles of the Civil War*. Greenwich, Conn.: Fawcett, 1955.

248

Monaghan, James. *Civil War on the Western Border, 1854–1865*. Boston: Little, Brown, 1955.

Myers, Frank. *Soldiering in Dakota*. Huron, Dakota: Huronite Printing House, 1888.

Nadeau, Remi. *Fort Laramie and the Sioux Indians*. Englewood Cliffs, N.J.: Prentice-Hall, 1967.

Nevins, Allan and Henry Steele Commager. *A Pocket History of the United States*. New York: Washington Square, 1967.

Nicolay, John G. *The Outbreak of Rebellion*. New York: Charles Scribner's Sons, 1881.

O'Donnell, Mayo Hayes. *Monterey's Adobe Heritage*. Monterey Savings & Loan Association, 1965.

————. "Peninsula Diary." *Monterey Peninsula Herald*. July 15, 1955 and June 1, 1970.

Oehler, C. M. *The Great Sioux Uprising*. New York: Oxford University, 1959.

Palfrey, F. W. *The Antietam and Fredericksburg*. New York: Charles Scribner's Sons, 1882.

Parkman, Francis. *The Oregon Trail*. New York: Farrar & Rinehart, 1931.

Pope, Maj. Gen. John. *Report of Operations in Virginia*. House of Representatives Executive Document no. 81, March 3, 1863.

Prucha, Francis Paul. *Broadax and Bayonet*. Lincoln: University of Nebraska, 1953.

Raymond, L. K. "Trip Over the Plains of Dakota in 1865." *North Dakota Historical Society Quarterly*, II, no. 3 (1928).

Returns from Regular Army Regiments. National Archives Microfilm Publication M665, roll 19, January 1854 to December 1860.

Robinson, Dr. DeLorme. "Editorial Notes on Historical Sketch of North and South Dakota." *South Dakota Historical Collections*, vol. 1, 1902.

Robinson, Doane. *A History of the Dakota or Sioux Indians*. State of Dakota, 1904.

Roddis, Louis. *The Indian Wars of Minnesota*. Cedar Rapids: Torch Press, 1956.

Ropes, John C. *The Army Under Pope*. New York: Charles Scribner's Sons, 1881.

Roske, Robert J. *Everyman's Eden: A History of California*. New York: Macmillan, 1968.

Sandburg, Carl. *Abraham Lincoln: The War Years*. New York: Harcourt Brace, 1939.

Scherer, James A. B. *Thirty-First Star*. New York: G. P. Putnam's Sons, 1942.

Sherman, William T. *Memoirs*. Bloomington: Indiana University, 1957.

Spaulding, Col. Oliver L. *The United States Army in Peace and War*. New York: G. P. Putnam's Sons, New York, 1937.

Spring, Agnes Wright. *The Cheyenne & Black Hills Stage and Express Routes*. Lincoln: University of Nebraska, 1948.

Sully, Gen. Alfred. "Official Report." *Army and Navy Official Gazette*, September 11, 1863.

Tebbel, John. *The Compact History of the Indian Wars*. New York: Hawthorn, 1966.

Utley, Robert M. *Frontiersmen in Blue*. New York: Macmillan, 1967.

U.S. Department of Commerce, Bureau of the Census. *Historical Statistics of the United States, Colonial Times to 1957*, 2nd ed. Washington, D.C.: Government Printing Office, 1961.

BIBLIOGRAPHY

U.S. War Department. *The War of the Rebellion: A Compilation of the Official Records of the Union and Confederate Armies*, series I, vol. XXII. Washington, D.C.: Government Printing Office, 1880–1901.

Ware, Capt. Eugene F. *The Indian War of 1864*. New York: St. Martin's Press, 1960.

Webb, Maj. Gen. Alexander S. *The Peninsula*. New York: Charles Scribner's Sons, 1881.

Wilhelm, Thomas. *History of the Eighth U.S. Infantry*. David's Island, N.Y.: Regimental Headquarters, 1871.

Williams, T. Harry. *Lincoln and His Generals*. New York: Alfred Knopf, 1952.

Credits

250

Index

The body text for *No Tears for the General* is set in Caledonia by CBM Type of Mountain View, California. The book was printed and bound by Kingsport Press, Kingsport, Tennessee.

Design by Arthur Andersen.